BETTY SAW'S
Best Noodle Recipes

Marshall Cavendish
Cuisine

The publisher wishes to thank Living Quarters (M) Department Stores Sdn Bhd, Parkson Corporation Sdn Bhd and New Convox Sdn Bhd for the loan of tableware used in this book.

Designer: Bernard Go Kwang Meng
Photographer: Pacino Wong of You Studio
Food Stylist: Maureen Tam
Food Preparation: Liou Chai Yen

Photo credit: www.123rf.com (page 3)

Published by Marshall Cavendish Cuisine
An imprint of Marshall Cavendish International

Other Marshall Cavendish Offices:
Marshall Cavendish Corporation, 99 White Plains Road, Tarrytown NY 10591-9001, USA • Marshall Cavendish International (Thailand) Co Ltd. 253 Asoke, 12th Flr, Sukhumvit 21 Road, Klongtoey Nua, Wattana, Bangkok 10110, Thailand • Marshall Cavendish (Malaysia) Sdn Bhd, Times Subang, Lot 46, Subang Hi-Tech Industrial Park, Batu Tiga, 40000 Shah Alam, Selangor Darul Ehsan, Malaysia.

Marshall Cavendish is a trademark of Times Publishing Limited

National Library Board, Singapore Cataloguing-in-Publication Data

Saw, Betty.
Betty Saw's best noodle recipes. – Singapore : Marshall Cavendish Cuisine, 2011.
p. cm.
Includes index.
ISBN : 978-981-4328-86-9

1. Cooking (Pasta) 2. Noodles–Asia. 3. Cooking, Asian. I. Title.

TX809.N65
641.822 -- dc22   OCN698502634

Printed in Singapore by KWF Printing Pte Ltd

DEDICATION

Dedicated with love to Saw Choo Boon

CONTENTS

INTRODUCTION

After having written 16 cookbooks, I have become lazy and devoid of inspiration to write another one. I am not short of recipes; I continue to take great interest in developing and trying out new recipes to delight my family and friends. However, my husband, who craves only for spicy food, complains that the recurrence of dishes he likes is few and far between.

When my publisher suggested I write a book on noodles, I thought it was a good idea. Putting together a book on noodles would not be a difficult task as I have numerous such recipes in my collection. I have done a lot of work on noodles mainly because my husband loves noodles, especially hawker fare. This book has essentially been a labour of love. In addition, with increasing health consciousness and lack of time among busy professionals, noodles, which long ago were only taken as snacks,

have become a popular replacement for rice in a meal. I find it very convenient to serve noodle dishes at short notice, especially when I have to entertain friends who simply turn up at my door.

Of course, there are elaborate noodle dishes like laksa, which takes time to prepare, but generally noodles are quick to cook and can serve as one-dish meals.

Noodles come in so many varieties and can be prepared in more styles than rice to suit all palates. They can be served in light soups, with a host of different gravies or sauces, or fried with various ingredients.

In this book, I have included recipes for every kind of noodles found in the region. I hope you will enjoy these dishes as much as my husband and friends have.

Betty Saw

WEIGHTS & MEASURES

Quantities for this book are given in Metric, Imperial and American (spoon) measures. Standard spoon and cup measurements used are: 1 tsp = 5 ml, 1 Tbsp = 15 ml, 1 cup = 250 ml. All measures are level unless otherwise stated.

LIQUID AND VOLUME MEASURES

Metric	Imperial	American
5 ml	$1/6$ fl oz	1 teaspoon
10 ml	$1/3$ fl oz	1 dessertspoon
15 ml	$1/2$ fl oz	1 tablespoon
60 ml	2 fl oz	$1/4$ cup (4 tablespoons)
85 ml	$2^{1}/_{2}$ fl oz	$1/3$ cup
90 ml	3 fl oz	$3/8$ cup (6 tablespoons)
125 ml	4 fl oz	$1/2$ cup
180 ml	6 fl oz	$3/4$ cup
250 ml	8 fl oz	1 cup
300 ml	10 fl oz ($1/2$ pint)	$1^{1}/_{4}$ cups
375 ml	12 fl oz	$1^{1}/_{2}$ cups
435 ml	14 fl oz	$1^{3}/_{4}$ cups
500 ml	16 fl oz	2 cups
625 ml	20 fl oz (1 pint)	$2^{1}/_{2}$ cups
750 ml	24 fl oz ($1^{1}/_{5}$ pints)	3 cups
1 litre	32 fl oz ($1^{3}/_{5}$ pints)	4 cups
1.25 litres	40 fl oz (2 pints)	5 cups
1.5 litres	48 fl oz ($2^{2}/_{5}$ pints)	6 cups
2.5 litres	80 fl oz (4 pints)	10 cups

DRY MEASURES

Metric	Imperial
30 grams	1 ounce
45 grams	$1^{1}/_{2}$ ounces
55 grams	2 ounces
70 grams	$2^{1}/_{2}$ ounces
85 grams	3 ounces
100 grams	$3^{1}/_{2}$ ounces
110 grams	4 ounces
125 grams	$4^{1}/_{2}$ ounces
140 grams	5 ounces
280 grams	10 ounces
450 grams	16 ounces (1 pound)
500 grams	1 pound, $1^{1}/_{2}$ ounces
700 grams	$1^{1}/_{2}$ pounds
800 grams	$1^{3}/_{4}$ pounds
1 kilogram	2 pounds, 3 ounces
1.5 kilograms	3 pounds, $4^{1}/_{2}$ ounces
2 kilograms	4 pounds, 6 ounces

OVEN TEMPERATURE

	°C	°F	Gas Regulo
Very slow	120	250	1
Slow	150	300	2
Moderately slow	160	325	3
Moderate	180	350	4
Moderately hot	190/200	370/400	5/6
Hot	210/220	410/440	6/7
Very hot	230	450	8
Super hot	250/290	475/550	9/10

LENGTH

Metric	Imperial
0.5 cm	$1/4$ inch
1 cm	$1/2$ inch
1.5 cm	$3/4$ inch
2.5 cm	1 inch

FRESH YELLOW NOODLES

Fresh yellow noodles are readily available from markets and supermarkets, but here is a recipe if you'd like to make your own.

Preparation Time: 45 minutes
Cooking Time: 10 minutes
Makes 1.2 kg (2 lb 11 oz) noodles

Plain (all-purpose) flour 600 g (1 lb 5$^1/_3$ oz), sifted

Salt 1$^1/_2$ tsp + 1 tsp

Alkaline water 1 Tbsp, mixed with 250 ml (8 fl oz / 1 cup) water

Cooking oil as needed

1. Sift flour into a large bowl and stir in 1$^1/_2$ tsp salt. Make a well in the centre and slowly work in the alkaline water. Work into a ball of dough and knead until smooth.

2. Roll dough out on a lightly floured work surface into a square. Divide into 4 portions.

3. Working with 1 portion at a time, roll out dough into a large, thin rectangle. Dust each piece of flattened dough with tapioca flour to prevent dough from sticking between the rollers. Pass through a noodle roller adjusting until you get the dough to your preferred thickness. Pass through a noodle cutter to get strands of your preferred width. Alternatively, roll dough out with a rolling pin, then fold into thirds and cut with a knife or pastry cutter.

4. Bring a large saucepan of water to the boil. Add 1 tsp salt and 2 Tbsp oil.

5. Blanch noodles for 3 minutes, then drain and place in a large bowl. Add 4 Tbsp oil and toss well to prevent sticking.

6. Use as required or leave noodles to cool before storing in plastic bags. The noodles will keep for several days in the refrigerator and up to 1 month in the freezer.

FRESH EGG NOODLES WANTON MEE

Preparation Time: 1 hour
Makes 1.2 kg (2 lb 11 oz) noodles

Eggs 4, each 75 g (2¹/₂ oz)
Water 2 Tbsp
Salt 1¹/₂ tsp
Alkaline water 1 Tbsp
Plain (all-purpose) flour 600 g (1 lb 5¹/₃ oz), sifted
Tapioca flour for dusting

1. Break eggs into a bowl and stir with a fork to break eggs, but do not beat. Add water, salt and alkaline water and mix well.

2. Sift flour onto a work surface and make a well in the centre. Pour egg mixture into the centre of the well and using a fork, mix flour into the egg mixture. Keep stirring and mixing until mixture becomes a sticky mass. Using your palms, fold and knead until all the flour is completely worked in. Leave dough to rest, uncovered, for 30 minutes.

3. Roll dough out into a thick long sausage and roll out flat. Cut into 4 rectangles. Dust with tapioca flour.

4. Working with 1 portion at a time, roll out dough into a large, thin rectangle. Dust each piece of flattened dough with tapioca flour to prevent dough from sticking between the rollers. Pass through a noodle roller adjusting until you get the dough to your preferred thickness. Pass through a noodle cutter to get strands of your preferred width. Alternatively, roll dough out with a rolling pin, then fold into thirds and cut with a knife or pastry cutter.

5. Use as required or leave noodles to cool and divide into serving portions and store in an airtight container. The noodles will keep for several days in the refrigerator and up to 1 month in the freezer.

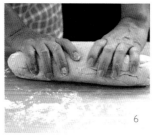

FRESH SPINACH EGG NOODLES

To obtain spinach juice, place a handful of chopped spinach (about 100 g / 3½ oz) and 2 Tbsp water into a blender and puree. Strain to obtain 2 Tbsp of spinach juice. For variety, celery or carrot can be used instead of spinach.

Preparation Time: 1 hour
Makes 1.2 kg (2 lb 11 oz) noodles

Eggs 4, each 75 g (2½ oz)

Spinach juice 2 Tbsp

Salt 1½ tsp

Alkaline water 1 Tbsp

Green food colouring a few drops

Plain (all-purpose) flour 600 g (1 lb 5⅓ oz)

Tapioca flour for dusting

1. Break eggs into a bowl and stir with a fork to break, but do not beat. Add spinach juice, salt, alkaline water and green colouring and mix well.

2. Sift flour onto a work surface and make a well in the centre. Pour egg mixture into the well and mix flour into egg mixture with a fork. Keep stirring and mixing until mixture becomes a sticky mass. Using your palms, fold and knead until all the flour is completely worked in. Leave dough to rest, uncovered, for 30 minutes.

3. Roll dough into a thick long sausage and roll it out flat. Cut into 4 long rectangles and dust with tapioca flour.

4. Working with 1 portion at a time, roll out dough into a large, thin rectangle. Dust each piece of flattened dough with tapioca flour to prevent dough from sticking between the rollers. Pass through a noodle roller adjusting until you get the dough to your preferred thickness. Pass through a noodle cutter to get strands of your preferred width. Alternatively, roll dough out with a rolling pin, then fold into thirds and cut with a knife or pastry cutter.

5. Use as required or leave noodles to cool and divide into serving portions and store in an airtight container. The noodles will keep for several days in the refrigerator and up to 1 month in the freezer.

RECIPES

BURMESE COCONUT NOODLES OHN-NO KHAO SWE

I first tasted this dish in Yangon when I visited Myanmar many years ago. It was lightly spiced and refreshing with a unique taste because of the dhal. I struck up a conversation with the chef and got an idea of the ingredients used, then reproduced my version of the dish when I returned home. This dish is great when you want a light meal.

Preparation Time: 1 hour
Cooking Time: 30 minutes
Serves 10

Dhal 150 g (5^1/$_3$ oz)

Minced chicken 600 g (1 lb 5^1/$_3$ oz)

Cooking oil 1 Tbsp

Fresh chicken or anchovy (*ikan bilis*) stock 3 litres (96 fl oz / 12 cups)

Thick coconut milk (*pati santan*) 250 ml (8 fl oz / 1 cup)

Salt 1^1/$_2$ tsp

Sugar 2 tsp

Fresh yellow noodles 1.2 kg (2 lb 11 oz)

Seasoning
Salt 1 tsp

Ground white pepper 1 tsp

Sugar 1 tsp

Corn flour (cornstarch) 1^1/$_2$ tsp

Paste
Onions 300 g (10^1/$_2$ oz), peeled and chopped

Garlic 5 cloves, peeled and chopped

Galangal 3-cm (1^1/$_2$-in) knob, peeled and chopped

Turmeric 3-cm (1^1/$_2$-in), peeled and chopped

Garnishing
Onion 1, peeled, quartered and thinly sliced

Chopped spring onion (scallion) to taste

Red chillies 4, seeded and sliced

Limes 8, small

Condiments
Thai chilli paste to taste

Fish sauce to taste

TIP
Fresh chicken stock is obtained from boiling chicken bones, chicken carcasses or breast meat over low heat for 1 hour. The stock is strained before use. Excess oil is skimmed off with a ladle. An easier way is to refrigerate the strained cooled stock until the fat has set on the surface and can be easily scooped out. Extra stock can be portioned and stored in plastic containers or bags for future use. They can be kept frozen for 4–6 weeks.

To make anchovy stock, heat ^{1}/$_2$ tsp oil in a large deep saucepan and fry 100 g (3^1/$_2$ oz) anchovies for a few minutes. Add 2 dried scallops and fry for a few more minutes. Pour in 3 litres (96 fl oz / 12 cups) water and bring to the boil. Simmer for 50–60 minutes. Strain and use as needed.

1. Start preparations a day ahead. Soak dhal in water and leave overnight.

2. On the day of cooking, season minced chicken with seasoning ingredients. Set aside for 1 hour.

3. Drain soaked dhal, then place in a food processor with 375 ml (12 fl oz / 1 1/2 cups) water and blend until smooth. Remove and set aside.

4. Combine ingredients for paste in a food processor and grind until fine. Heat oil in a deep pan and stir-fry paste until fragrant.

5. Add dhal and bring to a slow boil. Gradually pour in stock and return to a slow boil. Reduce heat and simmer, stirring until mixture is free from lumps.

6. Roll seasoned minced chicken into small balls and add to pan.

7. Stir in coconut milk, salt and sugar. Bring to the boil.

8. While chicken gravy is cooking, prepare noodles. Boil a large pot of water and scald noodles for a few minutes.

9. To serve, put some noodles in a bowl and top with chicken balls and gravy. Garnish with onion, spring onion, chillies and limes and serve Thai chilli paste and fish sauce on the side.

CHINESE MIXED VEGETABLE NOODLES

Preparation Time: 20 minutes
Cooking Time: 30 minutes
Serves 6

Skinless chicken thigh 450 g (1 lb), minced

Sugar 1 tsp

Salt 1 tsp

Ground white pepper $^1/_2$ tsp

Cooking oil 2 Tbsp

Shallots 3, peeled and sliced

Garlic 2 cloves, peeled and sliced

Soy bean paste $3^1/_2$ Tbsp

Potato flour 2 tsp, mixed with 1 Tbsp chicken stock

Fresh yellow noodles 500 g (1 lb $1^1/_2$ oz)

Bean sprouts 200 g (7 oz)

Carrot 1, peeled and shredded

French beans 75 g ($2^2/_3$ oz), cut diagonally

Chinese chives 50 g ($1^2/_3$ oz), cut into 3-cm (1-in) lengths

Seasoned Chicken Stock

Fresh chicken stock (page 20) 500 ml (16 fl oz / 2 cups)

Sugar 1 tsp

Salt $^1/_2$ tsp

Ground white pepper $^1/_4$ tsp

Dark soy sauce 2 tsp

Vinegar Sauce (combined)

Black vinegar 3 Tbsp

Cider vinegar 1 Tbsp

Garlic 3 cloves, peeled and sliced

Garnishing

Red chillies 2–3, sliced

Chopped spring onions (scallions) 3 Tbsp

Cucumber 1, shredded

1. Season minced chicken with sugar, salt and pepper. Set aside.

2. Heat oil in a pot and lightly brown shallots and garlic. Add soy bean paste and fry until fragrant.

3. Add chicken and stir-fry until meat changes colour and is lightly cooked.

4. Pour in seasoned chicken stock and bring to boil. Lower heat and simmer for 3–5 minutes.

5. Stir in potato flour mixture to thicken stock. Remove pot from heat and set aside.

6. Boil a large pot of water and scald noodles, bean sprouts, carrot, French beans and Chinese chives separately. Drain well and arrange on a large serving dish.

7. To serve, place noodles in a deep bowl and top with scalded vegetables. Spoon some chicken gravy over. Drizzle with 2–3 tsp vinegar sauce. Garnish with sliced red chillies, spring onions and cucumber if desired. Serve immediately.

FRIED HOKKIEN NOODLES

This is a favourite noodle dish for many. Omit pork fat for a healthier option.

Preparation Time: 20 minutes
Cooking Time: 30 minutes
Serves 2

Chicken or pork 100 g (3¹/₂ oz), cut into thin strips

Salt to taste

Ground white pepper to taste

Shelled small prawns (shrimps) 100 g (3¹/₂ oz)

Squid or cuttlefish 100 g (3¹/₂ oz), cleaned and sliced

Cooking oil 2 Tbsp

Shallots 3, peeled and sliced

Pork fat (optional) 120 g (4 oz), diced

Garlic 4 cloves, peeled and minced

Fish cake (optional) 6 slices

Chinese flowering cabbage (choy sum) 3–4 stalks, washed and cut into 5-cm (2-in) lengths

Fresh yellow noodles 480 g (1 lb 1 oz)

Lettuce leaves a few, shredded

Seasoning

Sesame oil ¹/₂ tsp

Ground white pepper ¹/₄ tsp

Light soy sauce ¹/₂ Tbsp

Sauce (combined)

Fresh chicken or pork bone stock 500 ml (16 fl oz / 2 cups)

Dark soy sauce 1 Tbsp

1. Season chicken or pork with salt and pepper.

2. Mix prawns with squid or cuttlefish and add seasoning. Mix well. Leave for 15 minutes.

3. Heat oil in a wok and stir-fry shallots until light brown and crisp. Drain and set aside.

4. Reheat wok and stir-fry pork fat if using until light brown and crisp. Drain and leave oil in wok.

5. Reheat wok and lightly brown garlic. Add chicken or pork and stir-fry until meat changes colour and is lightly cooked.

6. Add prawns, squid or cuttlefish and fish cake, if using, and toss well for 30 seconds. Add Chinese flowering cabbage and stir-fry for a few seconds.

7. Add noodles and toss for 2 minutes. Add combined sauce ingredients, stir and cover wok for 1 minute.

8. Remove cover and sprinkle in crisp-fried pork fat if using and shallots. Dish out and garnish with shredded lettuce. Serve immediately.

TIP
To make pork bone stock, place 2 kg (4 lb 6 oz) pork bones with some meat and 6 litres (192 fl oz / 24 cups) water into a large pot and bring to the boil. Skim off any scum that rises to the top. Simmer gently for 7 hours or until stock is reduced to about 4 litres (128 fl oz / 16 cups). Leave to cool, then discard bones and reserve meat. Strain stock to remove bone fragments. Store in plastic containers or bags for future use. They can be kept frozen for 4–6 weeks.

LAM MEE

This noodle dish is popularly eaten for lunch. It is easy to prepare and is deliciously wholesome. It is most appetising if served with sambal *belacan*.

Preparation Time: 30 minutes
Cooking Time: 30 minutes
Serves 8

Chicken or pork 180 g (6^1/$_2$ oz), cut into strips

Shelled prawns (shrimps) 120 g (4 oz)

Salt ^{1}/$_2$ tsp

Ground white pepper ^{1}/$_4$ tsp

Light soy sauce 1 tsp

Corn flour (cornstarch) 1 tsp

Bean sprouts 300 g (10^1/$_2$ oz)

Cooking oil 4 Tbsp

Chinese flowering cabbage (choy sum) 150 g (5^1/$_3$ oz)

Fresh yellow noodles 900 g (2 lb)

Shallots 3, peeled and sliced

Garlic 4 cloves, peeled and minced

Dried Chinese mushrooms 3, soaked to soften, stems discarded and cut into strips

Cooked crabmeat 55–85 g (2–3 oz)

Spring onion (scallion) 1, chopped

Red chillies 3, cut into thin strips

Gravy

Water or fresh chicken stock (see note, page 20) 1 litre (32 fl oz / 4 cups)

Light soy sauce 4 tsp

Dark soy sauce ^{1}/$_2$ tsp

Sesame oil 1 tsp

Salt 1^1/$_2$ tsp

Ground white pepper ^{1}/$_4$ tsp

Corn flour (cornstarch) 7 tsp

Sambal Belacan

Dried prawn (shrimp) paste (*belacan*) 5 x 5 x ^{1}/$_2$ cm (2 x 2 x ^{1}/$_4$-in) piece

Red chillies 8, seeded

Kalamansi limes 3, juice extracted

1. To make sambal *belacan*, roast prawn paste in a dry pan until fragrant. When prawn paste is still hot, pound it with chillies until smooth. Spoon into a small saucer and mix with lime juice.

2. Season chicken or pork and prawns separately with salt, pepper, light soy sauce and corn flour. Set aside.

3. Boil a large pot of water and scald bean sprouts. Drain and set aside.

4. Add 1 Tbsp oil to boiling water and scald Chinese flowering cabbage. Drain and set aside.

5. Reheat water and scald noodles for a few minutes. Drain and place into serving bowl. Mix with scalded bean sprouts.

6. Heat remaining 3 Tbsp oil in a wok and brown shallots and garlic. Add mushrooms and stir-fry for a while, then add seasoned chicken or pork and seasoned prawns.

7. Combine ingredients for gravy and stir well. Pour over ingredients in wok, then cover and allow gravy to come to the boil.

8. Remove cover and add crabmeat. Mix and quickly ladle gravy onto prepared noodles.

9. Top with Chinese flowering cabbage and garnish with spring onion and chilli strips. Serve with sliced chillies and sambal *belacan*.

LOR MEE

Preparation Time: 30 minutes
Cooking Time: 30 minutes
Serves 5

Chicken or pork 300 g (10½ oz), cut into strips

Shelled small prawns (shrimps) 450 g (1 lb)

Cuttlefish 300 g (10½ oz), cleaned and sliced

Salt 1½ tsp

Ground white pepper 1½ tsp

Light soy sauce 3 tsp

Cooking oil 4 Tbsp

Shallots 5, peeled and diced

Garlic 5 cloves, peeled and minced

Fresh yellow noodles 1 kg (2 lb 3 oz)

Black vinegar 4 Tbsp

Corn flour (cornstarch) 3 Tbsp, mixed with 125 ml (4 fl oz / ½ cup) water

Eggs 2, lightly beaten

Spring onions (scallions) 2, chopped

Coriander leaves (cilantro) 2 sprigs, chopped

Red chillies 3–4, seeded and sliced

Gravy

Fresh chicken or anchovy (*ikan bilis*) stock (see note, page 20) 1.5 litres (48 fl oz / 6 cups)

Carrot 1, cut into 5-cm (2-in) strips

Long Chinese cabbage 4 leaves, cut into 1.5-cm (¾-in) strips

Dark soy sauce ½ tsp

Fish balls 12

Sambal *Belacan*

Dried prawn (shrimp) paste (*belacan*) 5 × 5 × ½-cm (2 × 2 × ¼-in) piece

Red chillies 8, seeded

Kalamansi limes 3, juice extracted

1. To make sambal *belacan*, roast dried prawn paste in a dry pan until fragrant. When prawn paste is still hot, pound it with chillies until smooth. Spoon into a small saucer and mix with lime juice.

2. Marinate chicken or pork and prawns separately with ½ tsp salt, ½ tsp pepper and 1 tsp light soy sauce. Set aside.

3. Heat oil in a wok and brown shallots and garlic. Add seasoned chicken and stir-fry for 2 minutes, then add prawns and cuttlefish. Stir-fry until just cooked. Set aside.

4. Pour chicken or anchovy stock into wok and bring to a boil. Add carrot, cabbage leaves, the remaining light soy sauce, dark soy sauce and fish balls, and simmer for a few minutes.

5. Add noodles and bring to a slow boil over moderate heat, stirring in black vinegar, remaining salt and corn flour mixture. Pour beaten eggs over boiling gravy, stirring gently. Add spring onions and coriander leaves just before serving.

6. Serve immediately with sliced chillies and light soy sauce or sambal *belacan*.

MAMAK MEE GORENG

Mamaks are Indian Muslims from South India. Their style of cuisine is a hybrid of Chinese, Malay and Indian cooking. This delicious noodle dish is the result of the three culinary influences coming together in one plate.

Preparation Time: 30 minutes
Cooking Time: 30 minutes
Serves 4

Shelled small prawns (shrimps) 100 g (3^1/$_2$ oz)

Chicken fillet 100 g (3^1/$_2$ oz), diced

Salt ^{1}/$_2$ tsp

Sugar ^{1}/$_2$ tsp

Ground white pepper ^{1}/$_4$ tsp

Cooking oil 2 Tbsp

Onion 1, peeled, halved and sliced

Garlic 2 cloves, peeled and minced

Firm bean curd 1 piece, diced

Tomato 1 large, diced

Fresh yellow noodles 400 g (14 oz), scalded briefly in boiling water

Egg 1, beaten with ^{1}/$_2$ tsp ground white pepper

Bean sprouts 100 g (3^1/$_2$ oz)

Red chilli 1, seeded and sliced

Spring onion (scallion) 1, chopped

Kalamansi lime ^{1}/$_2$, seeded

Sauce (combined)

Light soy sauce 2 Tbsp

Dark soy sauce 2 tsp

Tomato ketchup 2 Tbsp

Salt ^{1}/$_2$ tsp

Sugar ^{1}/$_2$ tsp

Chilli Paste

Dried chillies 12, seeded and soaked

Red chillies 10, seeded

Dried prawn (shrimp) paste (belacan) granules 1 tsp, roasted

Salt 1 tsp

Sugar ^{1}/$_2$ tsp

Tamarind pulp 1 tsp, mixed with 2 Tbsp water and strained to get 2 Tbsp juice

Cooking oil 1 Tbsp

1. To make chilli paste, combine dried chillies, red chillies, dried prawn paste granules, salt, sugar, tamarind juice and oil in a food processor and blend until smooth. Pour mixture into a non-stick wok and cook over medium heat for a few minutes.

2. Season prawns and chicken with salt, sugar and pepper. Set aside.

3. Heat oil in a wok and fry onion until transparent. Add garlic and fry for a few minutes. Add 3 Tbsp chilli paste, mix well and add prawns and chicken. Stir-fry until prawns and chicken change colour.

4. Add bean curd and tomato. When tomato is softened, add noodles and stir-fry for over medium heat for a few minutes. Add combined sauce ingredients and mix well.

5. Make a well in the centre of the noodles and add beaten egg, scrambling the egg evenly until cooked through. Add bean sprouts, red chilli and spring onion, and stir-fry for a few seconds.

6. Squeeze kalamansi juice over noodles, mix well and serve immediately; garnish as desired.

TIP
The chilli paste in this recipe keeps well in the refrigerator for 3–4 days and over 1 month if frozen. Scalding fresh yellow noodles briefly before cooking gets rid of excess oil in the noodles. Do this just before cooking or the noodles may stick together if left to sit.

MEE BANDUNG

Although named after a town in Indonesia, you will not be able to find this dish in Indonesia. This dish is believed to have originated from Johor.

Preparation Time: 30 minutes
Cooking Time: 30 minutes
Serves 8

Chicken fillet 200 g (7 oz), sliced

Shelled prawns (shrimps) 200 g (7 oz)

Salt 1/2 tsp

Sugar 1/2 tsp

Ground white pepper 1/4 tsp

Sauce

Cooking oil 2 Tbsp

Onion 1, peeled, halved and sliced

Chopped garlic 3 Tbsp

Red chillies 2, seeded and finely ground with 3 bird's eye chillies (*cili padi*)

Tomatoes 4, cut into 1-cm (1/2-in) cubes

Fresh chicken stock (page 20) 2.5 litres (80 fl oz / 10 cups)

Chicken seasoning powder or granules 1 tsp

Salt 3 tsp

Sugar 2 tsp

Tomato ketchup 1 Tbsp

Cabbage 140 g (5 oz), shredded

Mustard greens 100 g (3 1/2 oz), cut into 5-cm (2-in) lengths

Potato flour 4 Tbsp, mixed with 8 Tbsp stock

Fresh yellow noodles 800 g (1 3/4 lb)

Garnish

Shallot crisps 3 Tbsp

Chopped coriander leaves (cilantro) 3 Tbsp

1. Season chicken and prawns with salt, sugar and pepper. Set aside.

2. Heat oil in a deep saucepan and lightly brown onion and garlic. Add ground chillies and stir-fry for a few minutes. Add chicken and prawns and stir-fry for a few more minutes until meat changes colour. Stir in tomatoes and cook for a few minutes. Pour in stock and bring to a boil.

3. Add chicken seasoning powder, salt and sugar to taste. Stir in tomato ketchup. Add cabbage and simmer for a few minutes. Add mustard greens and bring to a boil. Thicken with potato flour mixture.

4. Bring a large saucepan of water to a boil and cook noodles by scalding briefly. Drain and place noodles in individual serving bowls. Top with gravy and garnish with shallot crisps and coriander leaves. Serve immediately.

MEE GORENG

A simpler version of fried noodles cooked by Malaysian Indians from the South of India.

Preparation Time: 15 minutes
Cooking Time: 20 minutes
Serves 3

Dried chillies 12, seeded and soaked

Onions 2, peeled and sliced

Garlic 4 cloves, peeled

Cooking oil 4 Tbsp

Bean sprouts 140 g (5 oz)

Fresh yellow noodles 280 g (10 oz)

Egg 1, beaten

Shelled small prawns (shrimps) 140 g (5 oz)

Potato 1 large, boiled and cubed

Tomatoes 2, quartered

Tomato ketchup 2 Tbsp

Chilli sauce 1 Tbsp

Green chillies 3, seeded and sliced

Spring onion (scallion) 1, chopped

Cucumber 1/2, sliced

1. Combine dried chillies, 1 onion and garlic in a food processor and blend until smooth. Set aside.

2. Heat oil in a wok and fry the remaining onion until transparent, then add bean sprouts and stir-fry quickly for a few seconds. Add noodles and stir-fry for a few minutes.

3. Make a well in the centre of the noodles, add egg, prawns, potato cubes, tomatoes, salt, tomato ketchup and chilli sauce, and stir well.

4. Add blended ingredients to the wok and toss well. Just before removing from heat, add green chillies and spring onion. Garnish with sliced cucumber and serve immediately.

MEE REBUS

Preparation Time: 1 hour
Cooking Time: 1 hour
Serves 10

Chicken 200 g (7 oz), cut into thin strips

Shelled prawns (shrimps) 100 g (3^1/$_2$ oz), chopped into small pieces

Salt 1 tsp

Freshly ground black pepper ^{1}/$_2$ tsp

Coconut milk 2.5 litres (80 fl oz / 10 cups)

Sweet potatoes 1.25 kg (2^3/$_4$ lb), diced and steamed

Fresh yellow noodles 2 kg (4 lb 6 oz)

Bean sprouts 1 kg (2 lb 3 oz), tails removed

Hard-boiled eggs 6, quartered

Green chillies 6, seeded and sliced

Spring onions (scallions) 5, chopped

Kalamansi limes 12, halved

Dried chillies 20, seeded and soaked

Onions 3, peeled

Shallots 12, peeled

Garlic 5 cloves, peeled

Turmeric 6-cm (3-in) knob, peeled

Young galangal 3-cm (1^1/$_2$-in) knob, peeled

Freshly ground black pepper 1 tsp

Cooking oil 6 Tbsp

Soy bean garlic paste 2 Tbsp

Sugar 1 tsp

Salt 1 Tbsp

Chicken stock cube ^{1}/$_2$

Corn flour (cornstarch) 2 Tbsp, mixed with 4 Tbsp water

Prawn Crisps

Rice flour 100 g (3^1/$_2$ oz)

Plain (all-purpose) flour 55 g (2 oz)

Corn flour (cornstarch) 1 Tbsp

Coriander powder 1 tsp

Garlic 2 cloves, peeled

Lesser galangal (kencur) 3-cm (1^1/$_2$-in) knob, peeled

Candlenuts (buah keras) 5 whole

Salt 1^1/$_2$ tsp

Coconut milk 375 ml (12 fl oz / 1^1/$_2$ cups), from ^{1}/$_2$ grated coconut

Egg 1, beaten

Dried prawns (shrimps) (udang geraggau) 30 g (1 oz), diced

Cooking oil for deep-frying

1. To make prawn crisps, sift 3 types of flour into a bowl and add coriander powder, garlic, lesser galangal, candlenuts and salt. Combine coconut milk and beaten egg and blend well into mixture. Strain. Stir in diced dried prawns.

2. Heat oil in a wok for deep-frying. Drop 1 Tbsp batter onto the side of wok. Ladle oil over and when batter has set, ease it into the oil. Cook until golden brown. Drain crisps on absorbent paper and store in airtight container. Repeat until batter is used up.

3. Season chicken and prawns with salt and pepper. Set aside.

4. Blend coconut milk and sweet potatoes to form a paste. Set aside.

5. Combine dried chillies with onions, shallots, garlic, turmeric root, young galangal and pepper in a food processor and blend until smooth.

6. Heat oil in a wok and fry blended ingredients until fragrant. Add soy bean garlic paste and fry for a few minutes.

7. Gradually pour in gravy. Stir in sugar, salt and stock cube and bring to the boil. Add chicken and prawns and cook for a few minutes. If necessary, thicken with corn flour mixture. Bring sauce to a boil and turn off heat. Reheat again just before serving.

8. To serve, boil a large pot of water and scald noodles and bean sprouts separately. Drain and divide into individual serving bowls. Top with gravy and garnish with hard-boiled eggs, green chillies, spring onions and limes. Serve immediately with prawn crisps.

DRY PAN MEE

Preparation Time: 1 hour
Cooking Time: 45 minutes
Serves 6

Dough

Plain (all-purpose) flour 380 g (13$^1/_2$ oz), sifted

Salt $^3/_4$ tsp

Egg 1 large, beaten with a fork

Water 125 ml (4 fl oz / $^1/_2$ cup)

Chicken Mushroom Gravy

Chicken thigh meat 280 g (10 oz), skinned and minced

Light soy sauce 5 tsp

Salt $^3/_4$ tsp

Sugar $^3/_4$ tsp

Ground white pepper $^3/_4$ tsp

Potato flour 1 tsp

Dried Chinese mushrooms 4, soaked to soften and finely sliced

Sesame oil 1 tsp

Cooking oil 1 Tbsp

Shallots 2, peeled and sliced

Garlic 2 cloves, peeled and minced

Cloud ear fungus 12, soaked and shredded

Seasoning

Anchovy (*ikan bilis*) stock (page 20) 180 ml (6 fl oz / $^3/_4$ cup)

Oyster sauce 1 Tbsp

Light soy sauce $^1/_2$ Tbsp

Sesame oil $^1/_2$ Tbsp

Salt $^1/_2$ tsp

Ground white pepper $^1/_4$ tsp

Garnish

Shallot oil 2 Tbsp

Light soy sauce 2 Tbsp

Short-stem mustard greens 12, scalded

Spring onions (scallion) 3 stalks, chopped

Fried anchovies (*ikan bilis*) 3 Tbsp

Fried shallot crisps to taste

1. Place flour and salt in a large deep bowl. Make a well in the centre. Add egg and stir. Add water, one-third at a time, and mix and knead well to form a small ball of dough. Leave to rest for 30 minutes, covered with a damp tea towel.

2. Prepare chicken and mushroom gravy. Marinate chicken with half the soy sauce, salt, sugar and pepper and potato flour. Set aside. Meanwhile, marinate mushrooms with the remaining soy sauce, salt, sugar, pepper and sesame oil and set aside.

3. Heat oil in a wok and lightly brown shallots and garlic. Add mushrooms and stir-fry for a few minutes. Add chicken and stir-fry until meat changes colour. Add cloud ear fungus and stir-fry for another minute.

4. Combine seasoning ingredients in a bowl and stir well. Pour into wok and bring to the boil. Simmer for a few minutes. Remove and set aside.

5. Prepare *pan mee*. Place dough on a work surface lightly dusted with flour. Roll out to a 0.5-cm ($^1/_4$-in) thick rectangle. Cut into 6 portions.

6. Roll each piece of dough into a noodle or pasta machine until desired thickness is obtained. Use the second last notch on the machine. Alternatively, roll dough out with a rolling pin, then fold into thirds and cut with a knife or pastry cutter.

7. Cut each sheet into thin strips about 0.5-cm ($^1/_4$-in) wide. Dust with a little flour and gather into a neat bundle and set aside. Makes about 6 x 100 g ($3^1/_2$ oz) portions.

8. Bring a large saucepan of water to a boil and stir in $^1/_2$ tsp salt and $^1/_2$ Tbsp oil. Cook the noodles for 1 minute.

9. Drain and place noodles into individual serving bowls. Stir in shallot oil and light soy sauce. Top with mustard greens, chicken and mushroom sauce, a sprinkling of spring onions, fried anchovies and shallot crisps.

Photograph on page 42

PAN MEE SOUP

This is a popular hawker dish, served in soups or tossed with soy sauce, meat, anchovies and vegetables. *Mee hoon kueh* is associated with the Hokkien style of making the noodle by stretching and breaking the dough into pieces while *pan mee* is the Hakka and Cantonese version of rolling and cutting the dough into strips. *Pan mee* is typically made fresh, then cooked immediately to prevent sticking.

Preparation Time: 1 hour
Cooking Time: 1 hour
Serves 6

Dough

Plain (all-purpose) flour 380 g (13$^{1}/_{2}$ oz), sifted

Salt $^{3}/_{4}$ tsp

Egg 1 large, beaten with a fork

Water 125 ml (4 fl oz / $^{1}/_{2}$ cup)

Chicken Mushroom Soup

Whole skinless chicken thighs 2, thinly sliced

Salt 1 tsp

Ground white pepper $^{1}/_{2}$ tsp

Dried Chinese mushrooms 4, soaked to soften and shredded

Salt $^{1}/_{2}$ tsp + more to taste

Sesame oil $^{1}/_{2}$ tsp

Sugar $^{1}/_{4}$ tsp + more to taste

Ground white pepper $^{1}/_{4}$ tsp + more to taste

Cooking oil $^{1}/_{2}$ Tbsp

Shallots 2, peeled and sliced

Garlic 2 cloves, peeled and minced

Cloud ear fungus 15 g ($^{1}/_{2}$ oz), soaked to soften and cut into 2–3 pieces

Short-stem mustard greens 15, trimmed and scalded

Garnish

Fried anchovies (*ikan bilis*) 4–5 Tbsp

Spring onions (scallions) 3, chopped

Coriander leaves (cilantro) 3, chopped

Red chillies to taste, sliced

Light soy sauce to taste

Anchovy Stock

Cooking oil $^{1}/_{2}$ Tbsp

Anchovies (*ikan bilis*) 100 g (3$^{1}/_{2}$ oz), peeled and cleaned

Dried scallops 2, large, soaked and shredded

Water 3 litres (96 fl oz / 12 cups)

1. To make anchovy stock, heat oil in a large deep saucepan and fry anchovies for a few minutes. Add scallops and fry for a few more minutes. Pour in water and bring to the boil. Simmer for 50–60 minutes. Strain and set aside.

2. Place flour and salt in a large bowl. Make a well in the centre. Add egg and stir a little. Add water, one-third at a time, mix and knead well to form a small ball of dough. Leave to rest for 30 minutes, covered with a damp tea towel.

3. Prepare chicken and mushroom soup. Season chicken with salt and pepper and set aside. Season mushrooms with salt, sesame oil, sugar and pepper and set aside.

4. Heat oil in a large wok and lightly brown shallots and garlic. Add mushrooms and cook for a few minutes. Add cloud ear fungus and stir-fry for another minute. Add chicken and cook until meat changes colour.

5. Pour in prepared anchovy stock and bring to the boil. Reduce heat and simmer for 3 minutes. Add salt, sugar and pepper to taste.

6. Meanwhile, scald mustard greens in a small saucepan of hot water. Drain and set aside.

7. Prepare *pan mee*. Place dough on a work surface lightly dusted with flour. Roll out into a flat 1-cm ($^1/_2$-in) thick piece. Cut into 6 portions.

8. Roll each piece of dough into a noodle or pasta machine until desired thickness is obtained. Use the second last notch on machine. Alternatively, roll dough out with a rolling pin, then fold into thirds and cut with a knife or pastry cutter.

9. Cut each sheet into thin strips about 0.5-cm ($^1/_4$-in) wide. Dust with a little flour and gather into a neat bundle and set aside. Makes about 6 x 100 g ($3^1/_2$ oz) portions.

10. Bring a large saucepan of water to a boil and stir in $^1/_2$ tsp salt and $^1/_2$ Tbsp oil. Cook the noodles for 60 minutes. Drain and place into individual serving bowls. Top with mustard greens and spoon over hot soup.

11. Garnish with fried anchovies, spring onions and coriander leaves. Serve hot with a saucer of sliced of red chillies and light soy sauce on the side.

Photograph on page 43

DRY PAN MEE

PAN MEE SOUP

TERIYAKI SPINACH EGG NOODLES

Preparation Time: 20 minutes
Cooking Time: 20 minutes
Serves 3

Fresh spinach egg noodles 300 g (10½ oz)

Fresh chicken stock (page 20) 1.5 litres (48 fl oz / 6 cups)

Dried kelp (konbu) 1 piece, about 5-cm (2-in)

Dried bonito flakes 3 Tbsp

Instant dashi 1 sachet, about 15 g (½ oz)

Firm bean curd 3 pieces, fried and sliced

Dried Chinese mushrooms 3, soaked, shredded and seasoned with
   a pinch of salt, sugar and ground white pepper

Baby spinach 100 g (3½ oz)

White sesame seeds 1 Tbsp, toasted

Sauce

Light soy sauce 4 Tbsp

Sake 4 Tbsp

Mirin 4 Tbsp

Sugar 1 tsp

1. Combine ingredients for sauce and stir well. Set aside.

2. Boil a large pot of water, add salt and scald noodles for a few seconds. Drain and plunge noodles into a basin of cold water. Drain well.

3. Meanwhile, bring chicken stock to the boil in a separate pot. Add dried kelp, bonito flakes and dashi. Strain stock. Add sliced bean curd, mushrooms and spinach separately and cook for a few minutes. Remove from stock and drain well.

4. Add sauce to stock and bring to the boil.

5. Divide noodles into serving bowls. Top with bean curd, mushrooms and spinach. Sprinkle over with sesame seeds. Ladle stock over noodles and serve immediately.

COLD WANTON NOODLES WITH SESAME VINEGAR SAUCE

This spicy tangy noodle dish is ideal served for a light lunch. As it is eaten cold, it can prepared well ahead of serving time.

Preparation Time: 15 minutes
Cooking Time: 15 minutes
Serves 5

Garlic 3 cloves, peeled and finely chopped

Young ginger 1.5-cm ($^3/_4$-in) knob, peeled and finely chopped

Red chilli 1, seeded and finely chopped

Bird's eye chillies (*cili padi*) 2, seeded and finely chopped

Spring onions (scallions) 2, finely chopped

Salt 1 tsp

Fresh egg noodles 500 g (1 lb 1$^1/_2$ oz)

Cucumber $^1/_2$, peeled and shredded

Dressing

Black vinegar 4 Tbsp

Dark soy sauce 3 Tbsp

Thick sweet soy sauce (*kicap manis*) 2 Tbsp

Sesame oil 2 Tbsp

Chilli oil 1 tsp

Sugar 2 tsp

Salt 1$^1/_2$ tsp

Ground white pepper $^1/_4$ tsp

1. Combine garlic, young ginger, chillies, half the spring onions and all dressing ingredients in a screwtop jar. Cover and shake well to combine. Set aside.

2. Boil a large pot of water and add salt. Scald noodles for a few seconds. Drain and plunge into a basin of cold water. Drain well and divide among 5 serving plates.

3. Drizzle dressing over noodles and toss well. Garnish with shredded cucumber and the remaining spring onions and serve immediately.

DRY SPICY TOMATO CHICKEN NOODLES

This savoury noodle dish is a Malaysian version of the Chinese *cha cheong meen*, tweaked with a fresh, light, and tangy taste.

Preparation Time: 40 minutes
Cooking Time: 15 minutes
Serves 5

Red chillies 8, seeded

Dried prawn (shrimp) paste (*belacan*) granules 2 tsp

Shallots 5, peeled

Garlic 6 cloves, peeled

Salt 1 tsp

Water 4 Tbsp

Minced chicken 125 g ($4^1/_2$ oz)

Tomatoes 2, diced

Sunflower oil 5 Tbsp

Fresh chicken stock (page 20) 5 Tbsp

Sugar $1^1/_2$ tsp

Bird's eye chilli (*cili padi*) 4, seeded and chopped

Coriander leaves (cilantro) 2 sprigs, chopped

Spring onions (scallions) 2, chopped

Thai basil 35 leaves, chopped

Fresh egg noodles 500 g (1 lb $1^1/_2$ oz)

Cucumber $^1/_2$, peeled, cut into 2 rolls and shredded

1. Combine chillies, dried prawn paste granules, shallots, garlic, salt and water in a food processor and blend until smooth.

2. Toss blended mixture with minced chicken and diced tomatoes. Set aside for at least 30 minutes.

3. Heat oil in a wok and stir-fry chicken mixture over medium heat for a few minutes, or until mixture becomes thick.

4. Stir in chicken stock, sugar and bird's eye chillies. Bring to a boil and simmer for a few minutes. Stir in coriander leaves, spring onions and Thai basil. Set aside.

5. Meanwhile, boil a large pot of water and scald noodles for a few minutes or until just cooked. Drain and plunge into cold water. Drain well and divide into individual serving bowls. Top with chicken mixture and some shredded cucumber. Serve immediately.

FRIED WANTON NOODLES

If you have unexpected guests dropping by for lunch, you can try whipping up this quick and tasty dish. Dried egg noodles can also be used. Scaled them briefly before frying.

Preparation Time: 15 minutes
Cooking Time: 15 minutes
Serves 4

Chicken fillet 125 g (4$\frac{1}{2}$ oz), shredded

Shelled small prawns (shrimps) 100 g (3$\frac{1}{2}$ oz) or 1–2 dried scallops, soaked and shredded

Light soy sauce $\frac{1}{2}$ tsp

Sugar $\frac{1}{2}$ tsp

Ground white pepper $\frac{1}{4}$ tsp

Fresh egg noodles 400 (14$\frac{1}{3}$ oz)

Shallot oil 1 Tbsp

Cooking oil 2 Tbsp

Shallots 4, peeled and sliced

Garlic 3 cloves, peeled and minced

Dried Chinese mushrooms 4, soaked and cut into thin strips

Carrot 1, peeled and shredded

Chinese cabbage (*bok choy*) 4 leaves, cut into strips

Bean sprouts 280 g (10 oz), tails removed

Gravy

Oyster sauce 2 Tbsp

Light soy sauce 1 Tbsp

Fresh chicken stock (page 20) or water 2 Tbsp

Dark soy sauce 1 tsp

Salt 1 tsp

Garnish

Spring onion (scallion) 1, chopped

Coriander leaves (cilantro) 2 sprigs, chopped

Shallot crisps 1 Tbsp

Red chilli 1, seeded and cut into strips

1. Season chicken and prawns with light soy sauce, sugar and pepper. Set aside.

2. Boil a large pot of water and scald noodles for a few seconds. Drain and plunge noodles into a basin of cold water. Drain well again and place onto a dish. Stir in shallot oil and mix well. Set aside.

3. Heat oil in a wok and brown shallots and garlic. Add mushrooms and stir-fry for a few minutes, then add seasoned chicken and prawns. When chicken and prawns are cooked, add carrot and Chinese cabbage and stir-fry for a few minutes, then add bean sprouts. Add noodles and toss well.

4. Combine ingredients for gravy and stir into noodles. Using a pair of chopsticks, toss well until noodles are covered with sauce. Add spring onion and coriander leaves and toss lightly. Garnish with shallot crisps and chilli. Serve immediately.

KON LOH MEE WITH CHICKEN CHAR SIEW AND CHICKEN DUMPLING SOUP

Preparation Time: 1 hour
Cooking Time: 1 hour
Serves 6

Whole chicken thighs 3, skinned and de-boned

Shallot oil 1 tsp

Oyster sauce 2 tsp

Dark soy sauce 1 tsp

Fresh spinach or plain egg noodles 500 g (1 lb 1 1/2 oz)

Bean sprouts 30 g (1 oz)

Mustard greens 3–4 stalks

Char Siew Seasoning

Salt 2 1/2 tsp

Sugar 4 Tbsp

Light soy sauce 1 Tbsp

Dark soy sauce 1/2 Tbsp

Malt sugar (*mak ngar tong*) 1 Tbsp, combined with 2 1/2 Tbsp hot water and stirred until sugary

Red colouring (optional) 1/4 Tbsp

Chicken Dumplings

Minced chicken 125 g (4 1/2 oz)

Dried Chinese mushroom 1, soaked and coarsely chopped

Wood ear fungus 15 g (1/2 oz), soaked to soften and finely chopped

Water chestnut 1, peeled and chopped

Spring onions (scallion) 2, chopped

Salt 3/4 tsp

Sugar 1/2 tsp

Ground white pepper 1/2 tsp

Sesame oil 2 tsp

Corn flour (cornstarch) 1 tsp

Egg white 1 tsp, beaten

Wanton skins 24 pieces

Stock

Fresh chicken stock (page 20) 750 ml (24 fl oz / 3 cups)

Salt 1 tsp or to taste

Ground white pepper to taste

Sesame oil 1 tsp

1. Prepare *char siew* by lightly tenderising chicken thighs with the spine of a Chinese cleaver. Pat dry with paper towels.

2. Combine all ingredients for char siew seasoning in a large bowl and rub into chicken. Leave to marinate for 4–6 hours. Bake in preheated oven at 175°C (347°F) for12–15 minutes on each side or until just cooked through. Remove and cut into 1-cm ($^1/_2$-in) slices.

3. To make chicken dumplings, combine minced chicken, dried mushrooms, wood ear fungus, water chestnut and half the spring onions with salt, sugar, $^1/_4$ tsp pepper, 1 tsp sesame oil, corn flour and egg white. Mix well and set aside for 30 minutes.

4. Place a teaspoon of filling into centre of each dumpling skin, fold over to form a triangle and flatten slightly.

5. Boil a pot of water. Add salt and cook dumplings for a few minutes. Drain and place into serving bowls.

6. Meanwhile, prepare stock. Combine all ingredients for stock in a large pot and bring to a rapid boil.

7. Boil a large pot of water and scald bean sprouts and mustard greens. Drain and set aside.

8. Reheat water and scald noodles for a few seconds. Drain well and plunge into a basin of cold water. Drain well and place on top of bean sprouts. Toss well with the sauce.

9. Combine shallot oil, the remaining sesame oil, oyster sauce, dark soy sauce, the remaining pepper and 2 Tbsp stock in a serving bowl and stir well. Pour sauce over noodles and bean sprouts and top with chicken *char siew* and the remaining spring onions. Serve with chicken dumplings and stock on the side.

SAM SEE LOH SANG MEEN

Sam See is Cantonese for three shredded varieties. A family favourite for lunch, it is noodles bathed in delightful gravy accompanied by crunchy bites from ample bean sprouts. For this recipe, the pork fillet can be replaced with fresh scallops.

Preparation Time: 15 minutes
Cooking Time: 15 minutes
Serves 4

Dried Chinese mushrooms 4, soaked and shredded

Salt 2 tsp

Sugar 2 tsp

Chicken fillet 125 g (4¹/₂ oz), skinned and cut into thin strips

Pork fillet 125 g (4¹/₂ oz), cut into thin strips

Sesame oil 1 tsp

Salt 2¹/₂ tsp

Ground white pepper ¹/₂ tsp

Bean sprouts 125 g (4¹/₂ oz)

Fresh egg noodles 280 g (10 oz)

Shallot oil 1 Tbsp

Sunflower oil 2 Tbsp

Garlic 3 cloves, peeled and minced

Short-stem mustard greens 3–4 stalks, cut into 5-cm (2-in) lengths

Corn flour (cornstarch) 1¹/₂ Tbsp, mixed with 4 Tbsp chicken stock (page 20)

Red chillies 3, seeded and sliced

Light soy sauce 2 Tbsp

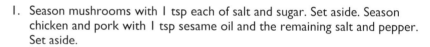

Gravy

Fresh chicken stock (page 20) 625 ml (20 fl oz / 2¹/₂ cups)

Light soy sauce ¹/₂ Tbsp

Salt ¹/₂ tsp

Sugar ¹/₂ tsp

1. Season mushrooms with 1 tsp each of salt and sugar. Set aside. Season chicken and pork with 1 tsp sesame oil and the remaining salt and pepper. Set aside.

2. Boil a large pot of water and scald bean sprouts. Drain and set aside on a serving dish.

3. Reheat water and scald noodles for a few seconds. Drain and plunge noodles into a basin of cold water. Scald noodles again in the pot of boiling water for a few seconds. Drain and place on a serving plate. Mix with scalded bean sprouts, add shallot oil and the remaining sesame oil, and toss well.

4. Heat sunflower oil in a wok and brown garlic. Add mushrooms and stir-fry for a few minutes, then add seasoned chicken and pork and stir-fry for a few minutes until the meat changes colour and is cooked.

5. Combine ingredients for gravy in a small pot and bring to a boil. Add mustard greens, stems first. When just cooked, return mushrooms and meat to the boiling sauce. Allow gravy to come to a boil, then add corn flour mixture to thicken.

6. Pour gravy over noodles and serve immediately with a sauce of sliced red chillies and light soy sauce on the side.

SESAME NOODLES

Sesame paste is nutty and aromatic in flavour. Adding it to this noodle dish transforms it into a special meal.

Preparation Time: 15 minutes
Cooking Time: 15 minutes
Serves 3

Cooking oil 1 tsp

Salt 1 tsp

Sugar 1 tsp

Bean sprouts 125 g (4$^1/_2$ oz), ends removed

Baby bok choy 6 stalks

Fresh egg noodles 300 g (10$^1/_2$ oz)

Shallot oil 2 Tbsp

Shallots 2, peeled and sliced

Garlic 2 cloves, peeled and minced

Fresh chicken stock (page 20) 180 ml (6 fl oz / $^3/_4$ cup)

Roasted peanuts 1 Tbsp, coarsely chopped

Roasted white sesame seeds 1 Tbsp

Chopped spring onions (scallions) 2 Tbsp

Sesame Sauce

Sesame paste 2 Tbsp

Light soy sauce 1$^1/_2$ Tbsp

Sugar 1 tsp

Sesame oil 1 tsp

1. Boil a large pot of water, add cooking oil, salt and sugar, and scald bean sprouts and baby bok choy separately. Drain and set aside.

2. Reheat water and scald noodles for a few seconds. Drain and plunge into a basin of cold water. Drain and set aside.

3. Combine ingredients for sauce and stir well.

4. Heat shallot oil in a small wok and lightly brown shallots and garlic. Add chicken stock and combined sesame sauce and stir well. Bring to a boil.

5. Place equal portions of vegetables and noodles onto serving dishes and top with sesame sauce. Sprinkle over with peanuts, sesame seeds and spring onions and serve immediately.

SINGAPORE TEOCHEW TAR MEE

When I am in Singapore, I never fail to visit the hawker centres for one of my favourite noodle dishes. It is a simple but very appetising noodle dish with well-paired meat ingredients and a delicious lightly spiced sauce that just clings to the noodles.

Preparation Time: 20 minutes
Cooking Time: 15 minutes
Serves 4

Minced pork or chicken 125 g (4¼ oz)
Salt ½ tsp
Ground white pepper ½ tsp
Light soy sauce ¼ tsp
Potato flour 1½ tsp
Lean pork or chicken 8 slices
Pork liver (optional) 8 thin slices
Fish balls 12, cooked
Cooking oil 2 Tbsp
Pickled garlic stems (*tang chai*) 30 g (1 oz)
Fresh egg noodles 450 g (1 lb)

Gravy
Chinese black vinegar 3 Tbsp
Light soy sauce 1¼ Tbsp
Sugar ½ tsp
Salt ¼ tsp
Ground white pepper ¼ tsp

Chilli Paste
Red chillies 3, seeded
Garlic 2 cloves, peeled
Shallot 1, peeled

Garnish
Fried dried sole 2–3, coarsely chopped
Chopped spring onion (scallion) 1 Tbsp

1. Prepare chilli paste. Combine red chillies, garlic and shallot in a food processor and blend until smooth.

2. Season minced pork or chicken with ½ tsp each of salt and pepper, soy sauce and 1 tsp of potato flour. Set aside.

3. Season lean pork or chicken and pork liver, if using, separately with the remaining salt, pepper and potato flour. Set aside.

4. Boil water in a large pot and scald seasoned meat and pork liver separately for a few seconds or until just cooked. Drain and set aside.

5. Using the same pot of boiling water, blanch cooked fish balls and set aside. Reserve 250 ml (8 fl oz / 1 cup) of water for later use.

6. Heat oil in a wok and stir-fry blended chilli paste until fragrant. Add pickled garlic stems and stir-fry for a few seconds. Pour in reserved stock and all gravy ingredients and bring to a boil.

7. Boil a separate pot of water and scald noodles for a few seconds. Drain and plunge noodles into a basin of cold water. Drain well. Divide noodles into serving bowls. Top with gravy, minced pork or chicken, lean pork or chicken, pork liver if using and fish balls. Garnish with dried sole and spring onions. Serve immediately.

SPICY EGG NOODLES

A noodle dish with a good bite of chillies and crunchy Sichuan preserved vegetables. Fresh or dried noodles work equally well.

Preparation Time: 15 minutes
Cooking Time: 15 minutes
Serves 4

Corn oil 2 Tbsp

Firm bean curd 2 pieces

Ginger 4 slices, peeled and chopped

Garlic 3 cloves, peeled and chopped

Red chilli 1, seeded and chopped

Sichuan preserved vegetables 100 g (3¹/₂ oz), finely chopped

Chinese cooking wine (Shaoxing) 2 Tbsp

Chilli bean sauce 2 Tbsp

Sesame paste or ground sesame seeds 1 Tbsp

Dark soy sauce ¹/₂ Tbsp

Sugar 1 Tbsp

Fresh chicken stock (page 20) 500 ml (16 fl oz / 2 cups)

Corn flour (cornstarch) 1 tsp, mixed with 1 Tbsp water

Bean sprouts 125 g (4¹/₂ oz)

Fresh egg noodles 450 g (1 lb) or 4 portions dried egg noodles

Spring onion (scallion) 1 stalk, chopped

1. Heat oil in a wok and stir-fry bean curd on both sides until golden brown. Remove, slice and set aside.

2. In the same wok, stir-fry ginger, garlic and red chilli until fragrant. Add preserved vegetables and stir-fry for a few minutes. Add Chinese wine, chilli bean sauce, sesame paste, dark soy sauce and sugar. Pour in chicken stock and bring to the boil. Reduce heat and simmer for a few minutes. Add corn flour mixture to thicken.

3. Boil a large pot of water and scald bean sprouts. Drain and set aside.

4. Reheat water and scald the noodles for a few minutes. Drain well and divide among 4 serving plates. Mix with scalded bean sprouts.

5. Ladle sauce over noodles and top with bean curd slices and spring onions. Serve immediately.

SPICY SICHUAN EGG NOODLES

This Sichuan version of sesame noodles is rather spicy. You can serve this dish as a meal by itself or dish out into smaller portions to serve with other Chinese side dishes.

Preparation Time: 20 minutes
Cooking Time: 15 minutes
Serves 4

Cooking oil 1 Tbsp

Sesame oil $^1/_2$ Tbsp

Dried scallops 2, soaked, drained and shredded; reserve water to add to chicken stock

Sesame paste 70 g (2$^1/_2$ oz), mixed with 4 Tbsp chicken stock

Chinese cooking wine (Shaoxing) 1 Tbsp

Fresh chicken stock (page 20) 750 ml (24 fl oz / 3 cups)

White sesame seeds 1 Tbsp, toasted

Peanuts 1 Tbsp, finely ground

Fresh egg noodles 450 g (1 lb)

Chopped spring onion (scallion) 1 Tbsp

Chopped coriander leaves (cilantro) 1 Tbsp

Chilli Paste

Dried chillies 3, seeded, soaked and sliced

Red chilli 1, seeded and sliced

Bird's eye chillies (*cili padi*) 2, seeded and sliced

Garlic 3 cloves, peeled and chopped

Sauce

Light soy sauce 3 Tbsp

Dark soy sauce $^1/_2$ Tbsp

Black vinegar $^1/_2$ Tbsp

Sugar 1 tsp

Salt $^3/_4$ tsp

1. Prepare chilli paste. Combine dried chillies, red chillies, bird's eye chillies and garlic in a food processor and blend until smooth.

2. Heat cooking oil and sesame oil in a wok and fry chilli paste until fragrant. Add shredded scallops and stir-fry for a few minutes. Add sesame paste and stir until smooth. Stir in Chinese wine and chicken stock and bring to a boil.

3. Combine ingredients for sauce and stir well. Pour over ingredients in the wok, then cover and allow gravy to come to the boil. Add sesame seeds and peanuts.

4. Meanwhile, boil a large pot of water and scald noodles for a few seconds or until just cooked. Plunge into a basin of cold water and drain well.

5. Divide noodles into serving bowls and top with gravy. Garnish with spring onion and coriander leaves. Serve immediately.

CLAYPOT CHICKEN MUSHROOM YEE MEE

A dry version of the soupy *yee mee* noodles served in a claypot. This makes a delightful weekend lunch for the family.

Preparation Time: 30 minutes
Cooking Time: 15 minutes
Serves 4

Chicken fillet 280 g (10 oz), skinned and minced

Salt 1 tsp

Light soy sauce 1 tsp

Dark soy sauce 1 tsp

Sugar 1 tsp

Ground white pepper 1 tsp

Potato flour 1 tsp + 1 Tbsp, mixed with 2 Tbsp reserved scallop water

Chinese cooking wine (Shaoxing) 1 Tbsp

Cooking oil 2 Tbsp

Pre-fried egg noodles 80 g (10 oz), about 1½ packets

Short-stemmed mustard greens 10 stalks

Dried Chinese mushrooms 5, soaked to soften and diced

Sesame oil ½ tsp

Shallots 2, peeled and sliced

Garlic 1 clove, peeled and minced

Dried scallops 4, soaked and shredded, 2 Tbsp of water reserved

Chopped spring onions (scallion) 1 Tbsp

Gravy

Light soy sauce 1 Tbsp

Oyster sauce 1 Tbsp

Salt ¼ tsp

Ground white pepper ¼ tsp

Sugar ½ tsp

Fresh chicken or anchovy (*ikan bilis*) stock (pages 20 and 28) 500ml (16 fl oz / 2 cups)

1. Season chicken with ½ tsp salt, light soy sauce, dark soy sauce, sugar, ½ tsp pepper and potato flour. Set aside.

2. Boil a large pot of water, add 1 tsp cooking oil and scald noodles for a few minutes. Drain and set aside.

3. Reheat water and scald mustard greens. Drain and set aside.

4. Season diced mushrooms with remaining salt, pepper and sesame oil. Set aside.

5. Heat the remaining cooking oil in a large claypot and brown shallots and garlic. Add seasoned mushrooms and stir-fry for a few minutes or until fragrant. Add shredded scallops and stir-fry for a few seconds, then add seasoned chicken.

6. Combine ingredients for gravy and stir well. Pour over ingredients in the wok, add Chinese wine and potato flour to thicken, then cover and allow gravy to come to the boil.

7. Transfer noodles to a large wok, pour in gravy and mix well. Return noodles to claypot and reheat a little. Arrange mustard greens on the side and sprinkle over with spring onion. Serve immediately.

KONG LAM MEEN

This splendid noodle dish has a delightful mixture of meat, seafood and mushrooms with gravy enriched with century and chicken egg. It is a very tasty and sustaining dish that is easy to cook.

Preparation Time: 30 minutes
Cooking Time: 20 minutes
Serves 4

Dried Chinese mushrooms 2, soaked and cut into thin strips

Chicken fillet 280 g (10 oz), shredded

Cuttlefish 1 medium, cleaned and sliced

Shelled small to medium prawns (shrimps) 100 g (3½ oz)

Salt 1½ tsp

Ground white pepper 1½ tsp

Light soy sauce 3 tsp + more to taste

Pre-fried egg noodles 280 g (10 oz)

Sunflower oil 2 Tbsp

Shallots 2, peeled and sliced

Ginger 2 slices

Garlic 3 cloves, peeled and minced

Dried scallop 1 large, soaked and shredded; water reserved

Chinese cabbage (*bok choy*) 3 large leaves, cut into 1-cm (½-in) thick slices

Fresh button mushrooms 6, halved

Enoki mushrooms 100 g (3½ oz), hard ends discarded

Young baby corns 2, sliced diagonally

Carrot 18 slices, peeled and parboiled

Sugar snap peas 10

Century egg 1, peeled and diced

Egg 1, beaten with a fork

Sesame oil 1 tsp

Potato flour 1 Tbsp, mixed with 2 Tbsp chicken stock or water

Spring onion (scallion) 1, chopped

Red chillies 4, seeded and sliced

Gravy

Fresh chicken stock (page 20) 750 ml (24 fl oz / 3 cups)

Light soy sauce 1½ Tbsp

Oyster sauce 1 Tbsp

Salt ½ tsp

Sugar ½ tsp

Ground white pepper ¼ tsp

1. Season Chinese mushrooms, chicken, cuttlefish and prawns separately with salt, pepper and light soy sauce. Set aside.

2. Boil a large pot of water and scald noodles for a few minutes. Drain and set aside in a deep serving dish.

3. Heat oil in a wok and lightly brown shallots, ginger and garlic. Add seasoned mushrooms and stir-fry for a few seconds, then add chicken and stir-fry until it changes colour. Add shredded scallops and stir-fry for a few seconds, then add cabbage, mushrooms, corns, carrot and peas.

4. Combine ingredients for gravy and stir well. Pour over ingredients in wok, then cover and allow gravy to come the boil. Stir in century egg and simmer for a few minutes on low heat.

5. Turn up the heat, then add beaten egg and sesame oil, and lastly add potato flour mixture to thicken.

6. Pour gravy over noodles and garnish with chopped spring onion. Serve immediately with a saucer of sliced red chillies and light soy sauce on the side.

SALMON NOODLES WITH PUMPKIN GRAVY

I first tasted this noodle dish at a chef-friend's restaurant. He is a creative chef full of good ideas. The naturally sweet and smooth pumpkin sauce is perfect for *yee mee*. Besides salmon, garoupa or threadfin fillet is just as good.

Preparation Time: 20 minutes
Cooking Time: 40 minutes
Serves 8

Salmon fillet 200 g (7 oz), sliced

Ground white pepper $^1/_2$ tsp

Freshly ground black pepper to taste

Cooking oil 4 Tbsp

Shallots 3, peeled and sliced

Garlic 3 cloves, peeled and minced

Pumpkin 1 kg (2 lb 3 oz), peeled and roughly diced into 1.5-cm ($^3/_4$-in) cubes

Anchovy (*ikan bilis*) or fresh chicken stock (pages 20 and 28) 1.5 litres (48 fl oz / 6 cups)

Salt $3^1/_2$ tsp

Sugar 1 tsp

Pre-fried egg noodles 280 g (10 oz)

Chinese cabbage (*bok choy*) 280 g (10 oz)

Fresh crabmeat with roe 100 g ($3^1/_2$ oz) cooked

Spring onions (scallion) 3 stalks, chopped

1. Season salmon with white and black pepper. Set aside for at least 15 minutes.

2. Heat oil in a wok and brown shallots and garlic. Add diced pumpkin and stir-fry for a few minutes, then add 500 ml (16 fl oz / 2 cups) stock and bring to the boil.

3. Reduce heat and simmer for 12 minutes, covered, or until pumpkin is soft.

4. Leave to cool, then place half the mixture into a food processor. Add salt and sugar and blend until smooth. Repeat with other half of mixture, then stir to combine.

5. Pour pumpkin puree into a deep pot, add the remaining stock and stir well. Bring stock to the boil. Stir in salmon and remove from heat.

6. Boil a large pot of water, add 1 Tbsp oil and scald noodles for a few minutes. Drain and set aside.

7. Scald Chinese cabbage in boiling water until just wilted. Drain and set aside.

8. Divide noodles into individual bowls. Top with pumpkin gravy, Chinese cabbage and crabmeat. Sprinkle over with spring onions and serve immediately.

FRIED MEE SIAM

This is the dry version of *mee siam* without the gravy. It is easier to prepare and good for quick meals.

Preparation Time: 45 minutes
Cooking Time: 30 minutes
Serves 8

Shelled small to medium prawns (shrimps) 1 kg (2 lb 3 oz)

Salt 1/2 tsp

Light soy sauce 1 tsp

Freshly ground white pepper a dash

Cooking oil 3 Tbsp

Coconut milk 375 ml (12 fl oz / 1 1/2 cups), from 1 grated coconut

Firm bean curd 6 pieces, cut into 0.5-cm (1/4-in) strips

Bean sprouts 280 g (10 oz), washed and drained

Chinese chives 140 g (5 oz), cut into 5-cm (2-in) lengths

Dried fine rice vermicelli 450 g (1 lb), scalded in boiling water and drained

Cucumber 1, peeled and shredded

Eggs 5, made into a thin omelette and cut into strips

Red chillies 2, seeded and sliced

Kalamansi limes 10, halved

Chilli Paste

Dried chillies 30, soaked in warm water

Shallots 240 g (9 oz)

Dried prawn (shrimp) paste (*belacan*) 2.5 x 5-cm (1 x 2-in) piece

Preserved soy beans (*tau cheo*) 3 Tbsp

1. Season prawns with salt, light soy sauce and pepper. Set aside.

2. Combine ingredients for chilli paste in a food processor and blend until smooth.

3. Heat oil in a wok and fry chilli paste until fragrant, adding 2 Tbsp coconut milk. Add prawns and a few more tablespoons of coconut milk, then add bean curd and stir-fry for a few minutes. Pour in remaining coconut milk, cover and allow gravy to come to the boil.

4. Add bean sprouts to the wok and mix well, then add Chinese chives. Lastly add vermicelli and toss well.

5. Divide noodles into serving plates and top with cucumber, omelette and chillies. Serve with limes.

FRIED RICE VERMICELLI WITH
BEAN SPROUTS AND WATER CHESTNUTS

A healthy, crunchy stir-fried rice noodle dish cooked without meat. It can be served hot or cold. For a vegetarian version, use vegetable stock instead of chicken stock.

Preparation Time: 20 minutes
Cooking Time: 15 minutes
Serves 4

Cooking oil 2 Tbsp

Garlic 6 cloves, peeled and finely chopped

Ginger 4 slices, peeled and finely chopped

Shallots 3, peeled and sliced

Spring onions (scallions) 6 stalks, cut into 3-cm (1½-in) lengths

Hot garlic bean paste (*taucu manis*) 1 Tbsp

Chilli bean sauce 1 Tbsp

Red chillies 4, seeded and finely shredded

Bean sprouts 280 g (10 oz), tails removed

Water chestnuts 10, peeled and finely shredded

Rice vermicelli 280 g (10 oz), soaked until soft and drained

Sauce

Light soy sauce 2 Tbsp

Dark soy sauce 3 tsp

Chinese cooking wine (Shaoxing) 2 Tbsp

Salt ½ tsp

Ground white pepper ¼ tsp

Sugar ½ tsp

Fresh chicken or vegetable stock (page 20) 125 ml (4 fl oz / ½ cup)

1. Heat oil in a wok and lightly brown garlic, ginger and shallots. Add the white parts of the spring onion, hot garlic bean paste and chilli bean sauce and stir-fry for a few minutes. Add chillies, bean sprouts and water chestnuts and stir-fry for a few minutes.

2. Combine ingredients for sauce and stir well. Pour over ingredients in the wok, then add vermicelli. Toss well for a few minutes until well combined. Sprinkle over remaining spring onions and serve immediately.

FRIED VEGETABLE RICE VERMICELLI

This is the ultimate fast food noodle fried in a wok. Although cooked only with vegetables, it is very tasty. To make it vegetarian, use vegetable and mushroom stock and serve with cut chillies and soy sauce.

Preparation Time: 20 minutes
Cooking Time: 20 minutes
Serves 8

Cooking oil 125 ml (4 fl oz / 1/2 cup)

Shallots 6, peeled and sliced

Garlic 4 cloves, peeled and sliced

Chinese cabbage 6 large leaves, cut into strips

Carrot 1, peeled and cut into strips

Bean sprouts 280 g (10 oz), tails removed

Dried fine rice vermicelli 500 g (1 lb 1 1/2 oz), soaked until soft and drained

Eggs 3, made into a thin omelette and shredded

Lettuce 1 small head, cut into strips

Red chillies 2, seeded and chopped

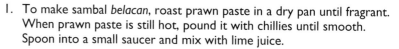

Sauce

Water 250 ml (8 fl oz / 1 cup)

Chicken stock cubes 2

Oyster sauce 2 Tbsp

Light soy sauce 2 Tbsp

Sugar 1 tsp

Ground white pepper 1/2 tsp

Salt 1/2 tsp

Sambal Belacan

Dried prawn (shrimp) paste (*belacan*) 5 x 5 x 0.5-cm (2 x 2 x 1/4-in) piece

Red chillies 8, seeded

Kalamansi limes 3, juice extracted

1. To make sambal *belacan*, roast prawn paste in a dry pan until fragrant. When prawn paste is still hot, pound it with chillies until smooth. Spoon into a small saucer and mix with lime juice.

2. Heat oil in a wok and brown shallots and garlic. Add cabbage, carrot and bean sprouts, then add vermicelli and stir-fry for a few seconds.

3. Combine ingredients for sauce and stir well. Pour over ingredients in the wok, then cover and cook over medium heat for 10 minutes.

4. Remove cover and stir-fry for a few minutes.

5. Divide noodles into serving plates and top with omelette, lettuce and chillies. Serve with sambal *belacan*.

FRIED VEGETARIAN RICE VERMICELLI

This classic Chinese vegetarian noodle dish makes a substantial meal in itself.
It is suitable for serving at a buffet or for bringing to a potluck gathering.

Preparation Time: 30 minutes
Cooking Time: 20 minutes
Serves 6

Cooking oil 750 ml (24 fl oz / 3 cups)

Dried sweet bean curd sticks 100 g (3¹/2 oz), rinsed and finely sliced

Sunflower oil 4 Tbsp

Dried Chinese mushrooms 4, soaked and cut into thin strips

Salt 1 1/4 tsp

Sugar 1/4 tsp

Ground white pepper 1/4 tsp

Sesame oil 1/2 tsp

Shallots 5, peeled and sliced

Cloud ear fungus 6, soaked and thinly sliced

Cabbage 450 g (1 lb), rinsed and thinly sliced

Carrots 2, peeled and shredded

Rice vermicelli 450 g (1 lb), soaked until soft and drained

Spring onions (scallions) 2, chopped

Red chillies 2, seeded and sliced

Sauce

Water 250 ml (8 fl oz / 1 cup)

Light soy sauce 2 Tbsp

Dark soy sauce 1 Tbsp

Salt 1 tsp

Sugar 1 tsp

Ground white pepper 1/2 tsp

1. Heat cooking oil for deep-frying in a large wok until hot. Add bean curd sticks and fry until crisp. Takes less than a minute. Drain and set aside.

2. Season mushrooms with ¼ tsp salt, sugar, pepper and sesame oil. Set aside.

3. Heat 1 Tbsp sunflower oil in a wok and brown 1 sliced shallot. Add seasoned mushrooms and stir-fry for a few seconds, then add cloud ear fungus and stir-fry for a few more seconds. Add cabbage and remaining salt and continue to stir-fry until cabbage softens. Set aside.

4. Reheat wok with the remaining sunflower oil and lightly brown the remaining shallots. Add carrots and stir-fry for a few minutes. Add rice vermicelli and mix well.

5. Combine ingredients for sauce and stir well. Pour over ingredients in the wok, cover and simmer for 5–6 minutes. Garnish with spring onions and sliced chillies.

INDONESIAN LAKSA

Laksa is basically a noodle dish served with coconut cream and spicy curry topped with a variety of meats or seafood and a tantalising array of fresh herbs. Almost every country in South East Asia has at least one version of laksa to tempt spice lovers. This lovely Indonesian variation is rich and creamy, thanks to the inclusion of coconut cream. It is tinged yellow with turmeric instead of bright red in the absence of ground chillies. Sliced chillies are sprinkled over the top to give a fiery bite. The gravy, enriched with chicken and fresh and dried prawns, holds all the fragrances released from the galangal, coriander, lemongrass, kaffir lime leaves and *salam* leaves.

Preparation Time: 1 hour
Cooking Time: 45 minutes
Serves 10

Whole chicken 1, skinned and halved

Salt 1 1/2 tsp + more to taste

Ground white pepper 1 1/4 tsp

Shelled small to medium prawns (shrimps) 280 g (10 oz)

Dried prawns (shrimps) 4 Tbsp, rinsed and finely ground

Cooking oil 3 Tbsp

Galangal 6-cm (1 1/4-in) piece, peeled and crushed

Lemongrass 4 stalks, smashed

Salam leaves 6

Kaffir lime leaves 8–10 pieces

Low-fat milk 1 litre (32 fl oz / 4 cups)

Fresh chicken stock (page 20) 1 litre (32 fl oz / 4 cups)

Coconut milk 2–3 Tbsp

Shallot crisps 3 Tbsp, crushed + more for garnishing

Dried fine rice vermicelli 800 g (1 3/4 lb), soaked until soft and drained

Spring onions (scallions) 4, chopped

Thick sweet soy sauce (*kicap manis*) 4 Tbsp

Kalamansi limes 10, halved

Spice Paste

Onion 1 large, peeled and finely sliced

Turmeric 10-cm (4-in) knob, peeled

Garlic 10 cloves, peeled and finely chopped

Dried prawn (shrimp) paste (*belacan*) granules 3 tsp

Candlenuts (*buah keras*) 12

Ginger 6-cm piece (3-in) knob, peeled

Lesser galangal (*cekur*) 3-cm (1 1/2-in) knob, peeled

Coriander powder 2 Tbsp

Garnish

Bean sprouts 280 g (10 oz), tails removed and scalded

Fried bean curd balls 10 pieces, shallow fried and quartered

Firm bean curd cakes 8 pieces, fried and sliced

Hard-boiled eggs 4, peeled and quartered

Red chillies 3, seeded and sliced

Green chillies 3, seeded and sliced

Bird's eye chillies (*cili padi*) 10, seeded and sliced

1. Season chicken with 1 tsp each salt and pepper and place in a heatproof dish. Steam over rapidly boiling water for 15–20 minutes. Cool and shred meat. Set aside.

2. Season prawns with remaining salt and pepper. Set aside.

3. Heat 1 Tbsp oil in a wok and fry dried prawns until fragrant. Set aside.

4. Combine ingredients for spice paste in a food processor and blend until smooth.

5. Heat remaining oil in a large wok and fry spice paste for a few minutes over low heat until fragrant. Add dried prawns, galangal, lemongrass, *salam* leaves and kaffir lime leaves. Stir well, then pour in low-fat milk and chicken stock. Bring to the boil, then cover and simmer for 15 minutes.

6. Add seasoned prawns, coconut milk, salt to taste and 3 Tbsp shallot crisps.

7. Meanwhile, boil a large pot of water and scald vermicelli. Drain.

8. To serve, place scalded vermicelli in individual bowls and top with garnish and shredded chicken. Pour over enough gravy to cover noodles and sprinkle with remaining shallot crisps and spring onions. Serve with thick sweet soy sauce and half a lime.

KERABU BEEHOON

This is a delicious Nyonya-style noodle salad that is appetisingly sour, spicy and fragrant.

Preparation Time: 30 minutes
Cooking Time: 20 minutes
Serves 4

Shelled small prawns (shrimps) 280 g (10 oz), diced

Cuttlefish 140 g (5 oz), cut into 2.5-cm (1-in) thin strips

Salt 1/2 tsp

Ground white pepper 1/4 tsp

Bean sprouts 280 g (10 oz), tails removed

Dried fine rice vermicelli 280 g (10 oz), soaked until soft and drained

Dried prawns (shrimps) 140 g (5 oz), rinsed and ground

Dried prawn (shrimp) paste (*belacan*) granules 1 Tbsp, toasted

Red chillies 15, seeded and blended until fine

Shallots 12, peeled and sliced

Lemongrass 3 stalks, tough outer layers discarded and sliced

Bird's eye chillies (*cili padi*) 15, seeded and sliced

Torch ginger buds 2, outer leaves discarded and sliced

Kaffir lime leaves 6, sliced

Basil leaves 20, sliced

Peanuts 3 Tbsp, toasted and coarsely ground

Sauce

Lemon juice 125 ml (4 fl oz / 1/2 cup)

Sugar 2 Tbsp

Light soy sauce 2 Tbsp

Fish sauce 3 Tbsp

1. Season prawns and cuttlefish with salt and pepper. Set aside.

2. Boil a large pot of water and scald bean sprouts and rice vermicelli separately for a few minutes. Drain well and set aside on a bamboo basket or colander to drain further.

3. Reheat water and scald prawns and cuttlefish. Drain well and set aside. Reserve stock for later use.

4. Heat a wok without adding oil and fry dried prawns until fragrant. Remove and set aside. Repeat with dried prawn paste granules. Remove and combine with dried prawns. Set aside.

5. In the same wok, add blended chillies and stir well. Allow paste to come to the boil. Remove and stir into dried prawn mixture.

6. Combine ingredients for sauce and stir well. Add shallots, lemongrass, bird's eye chilli, torch ginger buds, kaffir lime leaves and basil leaves. Mix well and stir in 4 Tbsp stock. Add more stock if you prefer the mixture to be more moist.

7. Add rice vermicelli and bean sprouts. Toss until well combined. Transfer noodles on serving dishes and sprinkle over toasted peanuts. Serve.

MEE SIAM TUA EE

My mum and her sisters are excellent cooks, but there is always a lot of rivalry among them, with each claiming to be the best cook, and guarding her recipes zealously. My cousins and I find it hard to differentiate between the dishes as we find them all very good. I have included two *mee siam* recipes here—one from my mum's eldest sister Tua Ee and the other from her youngest sister Choo Ee. Tua Ee's recipe is richer and less spicy, while Choo Ee's version (page 79) is spicier but less '*lemak*'. Although the two versions are rather different, I find both equally delicious. I leave it to you to judge.

Preparation Time: 1 hour
Cooking Time: 45 minutes
Serves 10

Cooking oil 4 Tbsp

Onions 3, peeled and finely chopped

Preserved soy bean
  paste (*tau cheo*) 140 g (5 oz)

Dried prawns (shrimps) 6 Tbsp,
  rinsed, pan-fried dry and ground

Tamarind pulp 70 g (2¹/₂ oz),
  mixed with 250 ml (4 fl oz / 1 cup)
  chicken stock (page 20) or water

Sugar 5 tsp

Light soy sauce 2 Tbsp

Fresh chicken or anchovy (*ikan bilis*) stock
  (page 20) 1 litre (32 fl oz / 4 cups)

Coconut milk (*pati santan*) 90 ml
  (3 fl oz / 6 Tbsp)

Kalamansi limes 2, juice extracted
  + 8 whole limes, halved and seeded
Shallots 4, peeled and finely chopped

Firm bean curd 3 pieces, halved
  and sliced

Fresh chicken stock (page 20)
  375 ml (12 fl oz / 1¹/₂ cups)

Bean sprouts 280 g (10 oz),
  tails removed

Chinese chives 100 g (3¹/₂ oz),
  cut into 3-cm (1¹/₂-in) lengths

Dried fine rice vermicelli 500 g
  (1 lb 1¹/₂ oz), soaked until soft and
  drained

Hard-boiled eggs 5, peeled and sliced

Red chillies 2, seeded and sliced

Spice Paste

Shallots 12, peeled

Garlic 4 cloves, peeled

Dried chillies 40, soaked and seeded

Dried prawns (shrimp) paste
  (*belacan*) granules 2 Tbsp

1. To make gravy, combine ingredients for spice paste in a food processor and blend until smooth.

2. Heat 2 Tbsp oil in a wok and fry spice paste for a few minutes or until fragrant. Add 2 onions and stir-fry for a few minutes until softened. Add preserved soy bean paste and stir-fry for a few minutes, then add dried prawns. Remove 5 Tbsp of fried ingredients and set aside.

3. Strain tamarind water and pour into wok. Add sugar, soy sauce and stock. Bring to the boil. Reduce heat and simmer for 10 minutes. Stir in coconut milk and lime juice, cover and bring to the boil. Remove and set aside.

4. Prepare noodles. Boil a large pot of water and scald vermicelli for a few minutes. Drain well.

5. Heat the remaining oil in a wok and brown the remaining onions and shallots. Add reserved fried ingredients and bean curd and mix well. Pour stock into wok and bring to the boil. Add bean sprouts and Chinese chives. Mix well. Add vermicelli and toss in the gravy to combine.

6. Divide noodles into individual bowls and top with hard-boiled eggs and chillies. Spoon over gravy and serve with kalamansi limes.

MEE SIAM CHOO EE

Preparation Time: 1 hour
Cooking Time: 45 minutes
Serves 10

Dried fine rice vermicelli 500 g
(1 lb 1½ oz), soaked for
10 minutes and scalded

Cooking oil 4 Tbsp

Dried prawns (shrimps) 140 g (5 oz),
rinsed, pan-fried dry and ground

Firm bean curd 6 pieces, halved and
sliced

Fresh chicken or anchovy (*ikan bilis*) stock
(page 20) 750 ml (24 fl oz / 3 cups)

Light soy sauce 4 Tbsp

Kalamansi limes 5, juice extracted
+10 whole limes, halved and seeded

Bean sprouts 500 g (1 lb 1½ oz),
tails removed and briefly scalded

Chinese chives 140 g (5 oz), briefly
scalded and cut into 2.5-cm (1-in)
lengths

Shelled medium to large prawns (shrimps)
500 g (1 lb 1½ oz)

Hard-boiled eggs 6, peeled and sliced

Red chilli 1, seeded and sliced

Spice Paste

Shallots 300 g (10½ oz), peeled

Dried prawn (shrimp) paste
(*belacan*) granules 2 Tbsp

Dried chillies 60, soaked and seeded

Gravy

Onion 1, peeled and sliced

Preserved soy bean paste
(*tau cheo*) 280 g (10 oz)

Coconut milk (*pati santan*) 125 ml
(4 fl oz / ½ cup), mixed with 2 litres
(64 fl oz / 8 cups) water

Sugar 30 g (1 oz)

1. Boil a large pot of water and scald vermicelli for a few minutes. Drain well and set aside.

2. Combine shallots, *belacan* granules and dried chillies in a food processor and blend until smooth. Heat oil in a wok and fry spice paste for a few minutes or until fragrant. Reserve 5 Tbsp for later use.

3. To the wok, add dried prawns and stir-fry for a few minutes, then add bean curd and stir-fry for a few minutes. Add stock and bring to the boil. Stir in 2 Tbsp light soy sauce, lime juice, bean sprouts and Chinese chives. Add vermicelli and toss well. Set aside.

4. Prepare gravy. Heat reserved spice paste and stir-fry for a few seconds. Add onion, then add preserved soy bean paste and stir-fry for a few seconds. Add coconut milk mixture and bring to the boil. Add prawns, cover and simmer for a few minutes. Remove prawns and place on a serving dish. Drain excess gravy into a saucepan. Stir in the remaining light soy sauce and sugar, cover and allow gravy to come to the boil.

5. Divide noodles into individual bowls. Top with sliced eggs and prawns and pour over enough gravy to just cover noodles. Garnish with sliced chillies and serve with kalamansi limes.

SARAWAK LAKSA

Amongst the various laksa dishes, Sarawak laksa is unusual due to its intense aromatic fragrance and taste. This is attributed to the use of mini coriander leaves available only in Sarawak. If mini coriander leaves are not available, they can be substituted with the larger variety, which is more easily available.

Preparation Time: 1 hour
Cooking Time: 1 hour
Serves 12

Dried prawns (shrimps) 100 g (3¹/₂ oz), rinsed

Water 3 litres (96 fl oz / 12 cups)

Sago or cider vinegar 2 Tbsp

Salt 1¹/₄ tsp + 2 Tbsp

Sugar 2¹/₄ tsp

Ground white pepper ¹/₄ tsp

Coconut milk 375 ml (12 fl oz / 1¹/₂ cups)

Anchovy (*ikan bilis*) stock granules 2 tsp

Shelled medium prawns (shrimps) 280 g (10 oz)

Dried medium strand vermicelli 500 g (1 lb 1¹/₂ oz)

Bean sprouts 500 g (1 lb 1¹/₂ oz), tails removed

Fish cakes 3, scalded, fried and sliced

Fried bean curd (*tau pok*) 6 squares, scalded, fried and sliced

Eggs 3, made into a thin omelette and finely shredded

Mini coriander leaves (cilantro) 3 bunches

Coriander leaves (cilantro) 1 bunch, chopped

Kalamansi limes 12, halved

Spice Paste

Cooking oil 4 Tbsp

Dried chillies 25, seeded and soaked

Shallots 300 g (10¹/₂ oz), peeled

Garlic 6 cloves, peeled

Dried prawn (shrimp) paste (*belacan*) 5-cm (2-in) square

Coriander leaves (cilantro) 2 small bunches

Coriander stems and roots 2 Tbsp, chopped

Coriander powder 1 Tbsp

Freshly ground black pepper ³/₄ tsp

Gravy

Sunflower oil 3 Tbsp

Dried chillies 20, seeded and soaked

Red chillies 3, seeded and sliced

Onions 4, peeled and diced

Lemongrass 3 stalks, sliced

Galangal (*lengkuas*) 3-cm (1¹/₂-in) knob

1. Combine ingredients for spice paste in a food processor and blend until smooth. Remove and set aside.

2. Place dried prawns in the food processor and blend until fine. Heat a wok and dry-fry blended dried prawns until fragrant. Remove and set aside. In the same pan, pour in the blended spice paste and fry over medium heat for a few minutes until fragrant. Add 250 ml (8 fl oz / 1 cup) water, vinegar, 1 tsp salt and 2 tsp sugar. Bring to the boil and simmer for a few minutes. Set aside.

3. Season prawns with the remaining salt, sugar and pepper. Set aside.

4. To make gravy, combine sunflower oil, dried and fresh chillies, onions, lemongrass and galangal in a food processor and blend until smooth. Pour gravy into a large wok and stir-fry for 10–12 minutes or until fragrant. Add remaining water and bring to the boil. Add coconut milk, salt and anchovy stock granules and prawns. Cover and simmer for about 5 minutes.

5. Meanwhile, boil a large pot of water and scald vermicelli and bean sprouts for a few minutes. Drain and set aside.

6. To serve, divide vermicelli and bean sprouts into individual serving bowls. Top with fish cakes, dried bean curd, egg, coriander leaves and lime. Pour over enough gravy to cover noodles. Serve immediately.

SINGAPORE-STYLE FRIED RICE VERMICELLI

Preparation Time: 20 minutes
Cooking Time: 20 minutes
Serves 4

Shelled medium prawns (shrimps) 15

Salt $1/4$ tsp

Sugar $1/4$ tsp

Freshly ground white pepper $1/4$ tsp

Dried fine rice vermicelli 280 g (10 oz),
   soaked until soft and drained

Shallot oil 1 Tbsp

Cooking oil 3 Tbsp

Ginger 5 slices, peeled and shredded

Eggs 3, beaten

Barbecued pork or chicken (*char siew**)
   280 g (10 oz), shredded

Onions 2, peeled and sliced

Red chillies 2, seeded and shredded

Meat curry powder 3 tsp

Bean sprouts 200 g (7 oz),
   tails removed and rinsed

Red capsicum (bell pepper) $1/2$,
   medium, cored and shredded

Chinese chives 100 g ($3^{1}/2$ oz), cut
   into 5-cm (2-in) lengths

Spring onions (scallions) 2, chopped

Sesame seeds 1 Tbsp

Coriander leaves (cilantro) for garnishing

Sauce

Water or fresh chicken stock
   (page 20) 250 ml (8 fl oz / 1 cup)

Chicken seasoning powder 1 tsp

Light soy sauce 1 tsp

Sugar 1 tsp

Salt 2 tsp

Ground white pepper $1/2$ tsp

1. Season prawns with salt, sugar and pepper. Set aside.

2. Boil a large pot of water and scald rice vermicelli for a few minutes. Drain and place on a dish. Stir in shallot oil and toss well.

3. Heat 2 Tbsp cooking oil in a wok and brown ginger. Add prawns and stir-fry over high heat until they change colour. Push prawns to the side of the wok and pour in eggs. Allow eggs to set slightly, then scramble. Add barbecued meat and stir-fry for a few minutes. Dish out and set aside.

4. Reheat wok with the remaining oil and stir-fry onions and chillies over high heat for a few minutes. Sprinkle in curry powder and mix well. Add bean sprouts and stir-fry for a few seconds. Return egg and barbecued meat mixture to the wok and toss well.

5. Combine ingredients for sauce and stir well. Pour over ingredients in the wok, cover and allow gravy to come to the boil.

6. Add rice vermicelli, capsicum and Chinese chives. Mix until well combined. Place noodles on serving dishes and sprinkle over spring onions and sesame seeds. Garnish with coriander leaves and serve immediately.

*For barbecued meat recipe see 'Kon Loh Mee with Chicken Char Siew and Chicken Dumpling Soup' recipe (page 50). For barbecued pork, cut into 3.5-cm ($1^{1}/2$-in) thick strips.

STEAMED FISH HEAD WITH RICE VERMICELLI

This is a healthy noodle dish with an appetising tangy gravy. Use a firm-flesh fish such as garoupa or red snapper and ensure that it is very fresh.

Preparation Time: 30 minutes
Cooking Time: 30 minutes
Serves 4

Fish head 1.5 kg (3 lb 4½ oz)

Salt 1½ tsp

Ground white pepper 1 tsp

Sesame oil 1 tsp

Shallot oil ½ Tbsp

Pickled sour plums 2

Pickled mustard cabbage (*harm choy*) 125 g (4¼ oz), soaked for 30 minutes and sliced

Dried Chinese mushrooms 4, soaked until soft and shredded

Roast pork or chicken meat 100 g (3½ oz), cut into 0.5-cm (¼-in) thick strips

Soft bean curd 2.5 x 5-cm (1 x 2-in), cut into 12 cubes

Ginger 5-cm (2-in) knob, peeled and shredded

Red chilli 1, seeded and shredded

Dried fine rice vermicelli 280 g (10 oz), soaked for 10 minutes and scalded

Short stem mustard greens 12, each about 10-cm (4-in) in length and scalded

Spring onions (scallions) 2, cut into 2.5-cm (1-in) lengths

Coriander leaves (cilantro) 3 sprigs, cut into 2.5-cm (1-in) lengths

Gravy

Cooking oil 1 Tbsp

Shallots 2, peeled and sliced

Garlic 2 cloves, peeled and minced

Dried scallops 2, soaked in 125 ml (4 fl oz / ½ cup) water and shredded; water reserved

Fresh chicken stock 750 ml (24 fl oz / 3 cups)

Salt 1 tsp

Light soy sauce 1 tsp

Ground white pepper ¼ tsp

1. Season fish head with salt, pepper, sesame oil and shallot oil. Squeeze and rub sour plums all over the fish. Place in a deep bowl and scatter pickled mustard cabbage, mushrooms, roast pork or chicken and bean curd all around sides of fish. Spread ginger and chilli on the surface of fish. Set aside.

2. To make gravy, heat oil in a wok and brown shallots and garlic. Add shredded dried scallops, and stir-fry for a few minutes or until fragrant. Combine chicken stock, salt, light soy sauce and pepper, and stir well. Pour over ingredients in the wok. Add reserved scallop water and bring to the boil. Reduce heat and simmer for 2 minutes.

3. Pour stock over fish head and place dish in a large steamer over rapidly boiling water. Steam for 20–25 minutes.

4. Meanwhile, boil a large pot of water and scald noodles and mustard greens separately for a few seconds. Drain and set aside.

5. Remove fish from steamer and sprinkle over spring onions and coriander leaves. Divide noodles and mustard greens into individual serving bowls and serve with fish head.

THAI FRIED CHILLI RICE VERMICELLI

The hot, sour and sweet taste of this Thai dish makes it most appetising.

Preparation Time: 45 minutes
Cooking Time: 30 minutes
Serves 8

Shelled small prawns (shrimps) or chicken 150 g (5⅓ oz), cut into 1-cm (½-in) cubes

Salt ½ tsp

Ground white pepper ¼ tsp

Cooking oil 5 Tbsp

Shallots 6, peeled and sliced

Garlic 4 cloves, peeled and sliced

Dried prawns (shrimps) 55 g (2 oz), rinsed and coarsely ground

Pickled radish (*chai poh*) 55 g (2 oz), finely chopped

Dried prawn (shrimp) paste (*belacan*) granules 1 Tbsp

Firm bean curd 3 pieces, sliced

Eggs 2, beaten

Bean sprouts 300 g (10½ oz), tails removed

Chinese chives 12 stalks, cut into 2.5-cm (1-in) pieces,

Spring onions (scallions) 3, cut into 2.5-cm (1-in) pieces + 2 for garnishing, chopped

Bird's eye chillies (*cili padi*) 10, seeded and chopped

Dried rice vermicelli 450 g (1 lb), soaked in water for 20 minutes until soft and drained

Roasted peanuts 3 Tbsp, coarsely ground

Chopped coriander leaves (cilantro) 2 Tbsp

Red chillies 1–2, seeded and thinly sliced

Sauce

Lemon juice 3 Tbsp

Fish sauce 4 Tbsp

Water 6 Tbsp

Sugar 2 Tbsp

Chilli Paste

Dried chillies 10, seeded and soaked until soft

Onions 2, peeled and cut into 2.5-cm (1-in) chunks

Garlic 6 large cloves, peeled

Dried prawn (shrimp) paste (*belacan*) granules 2 tsp

Dried prawns (shrimps) 55 g (2 oz), rinsed

Tamarind pulp 1 tsp, mixed with 4 Tbsp water and strained

Cooking oil 3 Tbsp

Brown sugar 1 Tbsp

TIP
If desired, prepare a larger portion of chilli paste and keep in the freezer for future use. This chilli paste freezes well and will keep for several weeks.

1. Combine ingredients for chilli paste, except brown sugar, in a food processor and blend until smooth. Heat blended chilli paste in a non-stick pan and fry over low heat for 8–10 minutes or until fragrant. Stir in brown sugar. Remove and set aside.

2. Season prawns or chicken with salt and pepper. Set aside.

3. Heat 4 Tbsp oil in a wok and brown shallots and garlic. Add dried prawns and pickled radish, and stir-fry for a few minutes or until fragrant. Add chilli paste and dried prawn paste granules. Add seasoned prawns or chicken and toss well until meat changes colour. Add bean curd and stir-fry for a few minutes.

4. Push ingredients to the side of the wok. Add 1 Tbsp oil and add eggs. Once eggs begin to set, scramble them until cooked.

5. Combine ingredients for sauce except the sugar and stir well. Pour over ingredients in wok and add sugar. Add bean sprouts, then Chinese chives, spring onions and bird's eye chillies and toss for a few seconds.

6. Add drained vermicelli and toss until well combined, cooked and dry.

7. Place vermicelli on a large serving dish and top with peanuts, spring onions, coriander leaves and chillies..

CHICKEN AND TRANSPARENT VERMICELLI SOTO

This delightful noodle dish has a rich spicy broth flavoured with a variety of aromatic herbs and spices.

Preparation Time: 30 minutes
Cooking Time: 30 minutes
Serves 6

Chicken thigh or breast meat 500 g (1 lb 1 1/2 oz), de-boned and skinned

Salt 1/2 tsp

Ground white pepper 1/2 tsp

Cooking oil 4 Tbsp

Coconut milk 250 ml (8 fl oz / 1 cup), from 1/2 grated coconut

Firm bean curd 3 pieces, fried and sliced

Transparent vermicelli 70 g (2 1/2 oz), soaked and scalded

Bean sprouts 280 g (10 oz), tails removed and scalded

Hard-boiled eggs 5, peeled and quartered

Shallot crisps 3 Tbsp

Garlic crisps 2 Tbsp

Celery leaves 5 stalks, chopped

Spring onions (scallion) 3 stalks, chopped

Red chillies 3, seeded and finely sliced

Bird's eye chillies (cili padi) 5, seeded and finely sliced

Kalamansi limes 5, halved

Ground Ingredients

Shallots 8, peeled

Garlic 4 cloves, peeled

Coriander powder 1 Tbsp, roasted

Candlenuts (buah keras) 5

Wild ginger root (cekur) 2.5-cm (1-in) knob, peeled

Dried prawn (shrimp) paste (belacan) powder 1 tsp

Turmeric powder 1 tsp

Stock

Fresh chicken stock (page 20) 1.5 litres (48 fl oz / 6 cups)

Lemongrass 4 stalks, mashed

Kaffir lime leaves 6

Galangal (lengkuas) 5-cm (2-in) knob, peeled and mashed

Salt 2 1/2 tsp

1. Season chicken with salt and pepper. Set aside.

2. To make spice paste, combine shallots, garlic, coriander powder, candlenuts, wild ginger root, dried prawn paste powder and turmeric powder in a food processor and blend until smooth.

3. Heat 2 Tbsp oil in a wok and fry spice paste over low heat until fragrant. This will take about 5 minutes. Remove and set aside.

4. Combine ingredients for stock in a large saucepan and bring to the boil. Add chicken, cover and allow stock to come to the boil, about 5–6 minutes. Remove chicken and drain well.

5. Add fried spice paste to the stock and simmer for 10 minutes. Add coconut milk and bring to the boil. Season to taste.

6. Meanwhile, heat 2 Tbsp oil in a wok and brown chicken. Cool, then shred.

7. Divide cooked vermicelli and bean sprouts into individual bowls. Top with fried bean curd, hard-boiled eggs and shredded chicken and sprinkle with shallot and garlic crisps. Pour over chicken stock. Garnish with celery, spring onions and chillies. Serve with limes.

FRIED TRANSPARENT VERMICELLI

A popular Hokkien noodle dish served at many Chinese restaurants. The transparent noodles, also known as glass noodles readily absorbs the flavours of the sauce. Use a good stock for the best results.

Preparation Time: 30 minutes
Cooking Time: 20 minutes
Serves 2

Dark soy sauce 1 tsp

Light soy sauce 2 tsp

Salt 1 1/2 tsp

Ground white pepper 1 tsp

Fresh chicken stock (page 20) 500 ml (16 fl oz / 2 cups)

Transparent vermicelli 125 g (4 1/4 oz), washed and drained

Chicken drumstick 1, de-boned and cut into strips

Shelled medium prawns (shrimps) 125 g (4 1/4 oz)

Corn flour (cornstarch) 1 tsp

Sugar 1/4 tsp

Cooking oil 4 Tbsp

Shallots 3, peeled and sliced

Garlic 2 cloves, peeled and finely minced

Ginger 2.5-cm (1-in) knob, peeled and cut into strips

Dried Chinese mushrooms 4, soaked to soften, drained and cut into strips

Red chillies 2, seeded and cut into strips

Spring onions (scallions) 2 stalks, cut into 2.5-cm (1-in) lengths

Coriander leaves (cilantro) 2 sprigs

1. Combine dark soy sauce, 1 tsp each of light soy sauce and salt and 1/2 tsp pepper in large bowl and stir well. Pour in chicken stock. Add noodles and leave to soak in stock for at least 30 minutes.

2. Season chicken and prawns with the remaining salt, pepper and light soy sauce, corn flour and sugar. Set aside.

3. Heat oil in a wok and brown shallots, garlic and ginger. Add mushrooms and stir-fry for a few minutes. Add chicken and prawns and stir-fry for a few minutes. Pour in stock and noodles and toss until liquid evaporates and mixture is almost dry.

4. Add chillies and spring onions and mix well. Garnish with coriander leaves and serve with sambal *belacan*, if desired.

TRANSPARENT VERMICELLI SALAD YAM WOON SEN

A standard offering in Thai restaurants, this sweet, sour and spicy salad makes a delicious accompaniment to any Asian meal. Do not overcook the noodles for that springy noodle texture.

Preparation Time: 30 minutes
Cooking Time: 15 minutes
Serves 4

Transparent vermicelli 450 g (1 lb), soaked

Shallots 100 g (3¹/₂ oz), peeled and sliced

Red chillies 15, seeded and sliced

Green bird's eye chillies (*cili padi*) 15, seeded and sliced

Garlic 7 cloves, peeled and finely minced

Pickled garlic (optional) 4 cloves

Fish sauce 4–5 Tbsp

Sugar 1 Tbsp

Kalamansi lime juice 125 ml (4 fl oz / ¹/₂ cup)

Minced chicken 200 g (7 oz), scalded

Cuttlefish 200 g (7 oz), thinly sliced and scalded

Onions 3 large, peeled and thinly sliced

Spring onions (scallions) 6, coarsely chopped

Coriander leaves (cilantro) 30 g (1 oz), coarsely chopped

1. Boil a large pot of water and scald vermicelli, leaving it in water for at least 2 minutes. Drain and plunge into a basin of cold water. Drain again and place in a large mixing bowl.

2. Add shallots, red chillies, bird's eye chillies, garlic and pickled garlic if using to the noodles, one at a time, mixing and tossing with two hands, using chopsticks.

3. Add fish sauce, sugar and lime juice, and toss well. Lastly, add chicken, cuttlefish and onions. Garnish with spring onions and coriander. Serve immediately.

FRIED MOUSE-TAIL NOODLES

This quick stir-fried noodle dish is often served in a claypot in Malaysia. Almost any ingredient, from fresh seafood to chicken, pork and ham can be added to this tasty dish.

Preparation Time: 20 minutes
Cooking Time: 15 minutes
Serves 4

Chicken thigh 1, skinned and diced

Salt $^1/_2$ tsp

Ground white pepper $^1/_4$ tsp

Mouse-tail noodles 500 g (1 lb 1$^1/_2$ oz)

Cooking oil 1 Tbsp

Shallots 3, peeled and sliced

Garlic 3 cloves, peeled and finely minced

Dried Chinese mushrooms 3, soaked to soften and diced

Turkey ham 70 g (2$^1/_2$ oz), preferably smoked, diced

Thick mustard green stems 3–4, cut into 0.5-cm ($^1/_4$-in) slices

Bean sprouts 200 g (7 oz), tails removed

Chinese cooking wine (Shaoxing) 2 Tbsp

Fresh chicken stock (page 20) 3 Tbsp

Shallot crisps 2 Tbsp

Spring onions (scallions) 2, chopped

Coriander leaves (cilantro) 2 sprigs, chopped

Sauce

Light soy sauce 1 Tbsp

Dark soy sauce 1 Tbsp

Thick sweet soy sauce (*kicap manis*) 1 Tbsp

Sugar $^1/_2$ tsp

Salt $^1/_2$ tsp

Ground white pepper $^1/_4$ tsp

1. Season chicken with salt and pepper. Set aside.

2. Boil a large pot of water, add a little oil and scald noodles for a few seconds. Drain and plunge into a basin of cold water. Drain well and set aside.

3. Heat a wok with oil and brown shallots and garlic. Add mushrooms and chicken and stir-fry for a few minutes. When chicken changes colour, add turkey ham and toss for a few seconds. Add mustard greens, bean sprouts and Chinese wine. Toss well.

4. Combine ingredients for sauce and stir well.

5. Add noodles to the wok and pour sauce over noodles. Stir-fry for a few minutes. Add chicken stock and stir-fry until liquid evaporates. Transfer to a serving dish and sprinkle with shallot crisps, spring onions and coriander leaves. Serve immediately.

LAKSA JOHOR

This is another favourite laksa dish. The rich, robust and fragrant gravy is due to the addition of roasted ground coconut (*keriseh*) and generous portions of fish.

Preparation Time: 1 hour
Cooking Time: 1 hour
Serves 12

Anchovy (*ikan bilis*) stock (page 20) 4 litres (128 fl oz / 16 cups)

Curry powder 10 Tbsp

Lemongrass 3 stalks, sliced

Laksa leaves (*daun kesom*) 12 stalks

Torch ginger buds 2, outer leaves discarded and sliced

Dried sour fruit slices (*asam gelugor*) 3 pieces

Shallots 15, peeled and sliced

Onions 6, peeled and finely sliced

Garlic 6 cloves, peeled and finely minced

Galangal 2.5-cm (1-in) knob

Ginger 2.5-cm (1-in) knob

Dried prawn (shrimp) paste (*belacan*) 5-cm (2-in) piece

Dried prawns (shrimps) 3 Tbsp, rinsed

Anchovies (*ikan bilis*) 280 g (10 oz), fried

Grated coconut 3 Tbsp, fried until golden brown

Mackerel fillets 6, steamed and flaked

Coconut milk 500 ml (16 fl oz / 2 cups), from 2 coconuts

Salt 3 tsp or to taste

Fresh rice noodles or spaghetti 1.5 kg (3 lb 4¹/₂ oz)

Garnish

Long beans 10–12 stalks, cut into 2.5-cm (1-in) lengths

Cucumber 1, peeled and shredded

Torch ginger buds 2, outer leaves discarded and sliced

Bean sprouts 300 g (10¹/₂ oz), tails removed and scalded

Preserved radish (*chai poh*) 2 Tbsp, chopped

Kalamansi limes 8–10, halved

1. Combine anchovy stock, curry powder, 1 lemongrass, laksa leaves, 2 torch ginger buds and dried sour fruit slices in a large pot and bring to the boil.

2. Combine shallots, 3 onions, garlic, galangal, ginger, the remaining lemongrass and dried prawn paste in a food processor and blend until smooth. Remove and set aside.

3. Combine dried prawns and fried anchovies in a food processor and blend until smooth.

4. Combine ground prawn and anchovy mixture with spice paste and fried grated coconut in a pot, cover and simmer over low heat for 30 minutes. Add fish, coconut milk and salt to taste.

5. Meanwhile, boil a large pot of water and scald noodles or cook spaghetti according to packet instructions. Drain and plunge into a basin of cold water.

6. Reheat water and scald long beans. Drain and set aside.

7. Divide noodles into individual bowls, pour over gravy and top with long beans, the remaining onions and torch ginger buds, cucumber, bean sprouts and preserved radish. Serve with limes.

NYONYA CURRY LAKSA

Nyonya curry laksa is another Malaysian favourite consisting of rich coconut gravy.
Its unique taste is due to the addition of fragrant dried prawns.

Preparation Time: 1 hour
Cooking Time: 1 hour
Serves 12

Cooking oil 125 ml (4 fl oz / ½ cup)

Large prawns (shrimps) 1 kg (2 lb 3 oz), eyes and feelers removed

Coconut milk 4 litres (128 fl oz / 16 cups), from 2 grated coconuts

Fish cakes 3, sliced

Anchovy (*ikan bilis*) stock granules 1 tsp

Salt 2 tsp or to taste

Rice noodles 1.5 kg (3 lb 4½ oz)

Spice Paste

Shallots 300 g (10½ oz), peeled

Onions 300 g (10½ oz), peeled

Turmeric 6-cm (3-in) knob

Dried chillies 30, seeded, cut into pieces and soaked

Red chillies 6, seeded

Dried prawn (shrimp) paste (*belacan*) 4 x 5-cm (1½ x 2-in)

Candlenuts (*buah keras*) 12

Lemongrass 6 stalks, sliced

Galangal 2.5 x 5-cm (1 x 2-in) knob, peeled

Dried prawns (shrimps) 60 g (2 oz), rinsed, coarsely ground and toasted

Garnish

Bean sprouts 600 g (21 oz), tails removed

Cucumbers 2, peeled and shredded

Mint leaves 2 bunches

1. Combine ingredients for spice paste in a food processor and blend
   until smooth.

2. Heat oil in a wok and fry spice paste for a few minutes until fragrant.
   Add prawns and stir-fry for a few minutes or until prawns are just
   cooked. Remove prawns and set aside.

3. Pour coconut milk into the wok, then cover and allow gravy to come to
   the boil. Add fish cakes. When gravy returns to the boil, return prawns to
   the wok. Add anchovy stock granules and salt to taste.

4. Boil a large pot of water and scald noodles and bean sprouts separately.
   Drain.

5. Divide noodles and bean sprouts into individual serving bowls.
   Pour over gravy and top with prawns, cucumbers and mint leaves.
   Serve immediately.

SALMON NOODLES WITH SPICY TOMATO GRAVY

This nutritious noodle dish consists of piquant tomato gravy, making it a refreshing and light accompaniment to the oily and rich flavour of the salmon.

Preparation Time: 1 hour
Cooking Time: 30 minutes
Serves 12

Salmon fillet 500 g (1 lb 1¹/₂ oz), cut into 1 × 4-cm (¹/₂ × 1¹/₂-in) pieces

Salt 1 tsp

Ground white pepper ¹/₂ tsp

Freshly ground black pepper to taste

Sunflower oil 2¹/₂ Tbsp

Tomatoes 14, skinned, roughly chopped and pureed

Fresh chicken or anchovy (*ikan bilis*) stock (page 20) 1.9 litres (64 fl oz / 8 cups)

Fresh thick rice noodles 2 kg (4 lb 6 oz)

Bean sprouts 450 g (1 lb), tails removed

White cabbage 140 g (5 oz), shredded

Garlic 1 clove, peeled and minced

Salted cabbage 140 g (5 oz), shredded, soaked and drained

Spring onions (scallions) 4, chopped

Red chillies 4, seeded and sliced

Kalamansi limes 6, quartered

Spice Paste

Red chillies 10, seeded

Bird's eye chillies (*cili padi*) 3, seeded

Garlic 10 cloves, peeled and minced

Shallots 8, peeled

Galangal 4 slices

Lemongrass 2, sliced

Turmeric 2.5 × 4-cm (1 × 1¹/₂-in) knob, peeled

Preserved soy bean paste (*tau cheo*) 4 tsp

Sauce

Fish sauce 4 Tbsp

Light soy sauce 2 Tbsp

Sugar 3 tsp

Salt 2 tsp or to taste

1. Season salmon with $1/2$ tsp salt and pepper. Set aside.

2. Combine ingredients for spice paste in a food processor and blend until smooth.

3. To prepare tomato gravy, heat 2 Tbsp oil in a wok and fry spice paste until fragrant. Add pureed tomato and stock, and stir well. Cover wok and allow gravy to come to the boil. Reduce heat and simmer for 10–12 minutes.

4. Meanwhile, combine ingredients for sauce and stir well. Pour into wok, then cover and allow gravy to come to the boil again. Add salmon and simmer for a few minutes. Remove from heat.

5. Boil a large pot of water and stir in the remaining salt. Scald noodles for a few seconds, drain and rinse in cold water. Drain and set aside.

6. Reheat water and scald bean sprouts and white cabbage separately. Drain and set aside.

7. Heat a small pan with the remaining oil and brown garlic. Add salted cabbage and stir-fry for a few minutes. Remove and set aside.

8. Divide noodles, bean sprouts, white cabbage and prepared salted cabbage into individual serving bowls. Spoon over gravy and garnish with spring onions, chillies and limes.

THAI LAKSA

This Thai laksa has a gravy made with coconut milk and the unique fragrance of lemongrass and sweet basil.

Preparation Time: 1 hour
Cooking Time: 1 hour
Serves 15

Mackerel 3 kg (6 lb 9 oz), cleaned

Salt 2 tsp

Cooking oil 4 Tbsp

Anchovies (*ikan bilis*) 280 g (10 oz), soaked and drained

Water 1.5 litres (48 fl oz / 6 cups)

Torch ginger buds 2–3, outer leaves discarded and finely sliced

Tamarind pulp 2 Tbsp, mixed with 250 ml (8 fl oz / 1 cup) water and strained

Fish sauce 1 Tbsp

Coconut milk 2.5 litres (80 fl oz / 10 cups)

Thai basil leaves 10–12 stalks

Coconut cream (*pati santan*) 500 ml (16 fl oz / 2 cups)

Fresh thick rice noodles 2 kg (4 lb 6 oz), scalded

Shallot oil 2 Tbsp

Bean sprouts 500 g (1 lb 1 1/2 oz), tails removed and scalded

Cucumbers 2, peeled and shredded

Mint 1–2 bunches

Ground Ingredients A

Dried chillies 30, seeded and soaked

Fresh red chillies 8, seeded

Turmeric 10-cm (4-in) knob, peeled

Ground Ingredients B

Shallots 30–35, peeled

Garlic 1 bulb, peeled

Candlenuts (*buah keras*) 10

Lemongrass 10 stalks, retain outer hard portions for boiling with anchovy stock

1. Rub fish with salt and steam over rapid boiling water for 10 minutes. When cool enough to handle, de-bone fish.

2. Heat 2 Tbsp oil in a wok and fry anchovies for a few minutes. Add water and torch ginger buds, then add outer hard portions of lemongrass. Cover wok and allow stock to come to the boil. Reduce heat and simmer for 30 minutes. Strain and set aside.

3. Combine ground ingredients A in a food processor and blend until smooth. Remove and set aside.

4. Combine ground ingredients B in a food processor and blend until smooth. Remove and set aside.

5. Heat the remaining oil and stir-fry ground ingredients A for a few minutes. Add ground ingredients B and stir-fry until fragrant.

6. Pour in prepared stock and tamarind juice. Add fish sauce and bring to the boil. Add coconut milk and when it begins to boil, add basil leaves. Simmer for 5–10 minutes. Add fish meat, coconut cream and salt to taste.

7. Boil a large pot of water and scald noodles. Drain well and stir in shallot oil. Divide noodles and bean sprouts into serving bowls. Ladle over gravy and top with cucumbers and mint.

FRIED KWAY TEOW WITH COCKLES

This dish is one of the most popular hawker dishes in Malaysia. The best fried *kway teow* has an appealing smoky flavour. To achieve this, a hot wok over high heat is essential.

Preparation Time: 15 minutes
Cooking Time: 10 minutes
Serves 3

Cockles 280 g (10 oz)

Shelled small prawns (shrimps) 140 g (5 oz)

Salt 1/2 tsp

Ground white pepper 1/4 tsp + more to taste

Cooking oil 4 Tbsp

Garlic 4 cloves, peeled and finely chopped

Ground chilli paste (*cili boh*) 1 Tbsp

Fresh flat rice noodles 500 g (1 lb 1 1/2 oz)

Chinese chives 3 stalks, cut into 2.5-cm (1-in) lengths

Bean sprouts 140 g (5 oz), tails removed

Thick sweet soy sauce (*kicap manis*) 1 Tbsp

Light soy sauce 2 Tbsp

Sugar 1/2 tsp

Eggs 2

Water 4 Tbsp

1. Boil a large pot of water. Place cockles in a large bowl and pour over boiling water. Drain immediately. Remove flesh from shells and set aside.

2. Season prawns with salt and pepper. Set aside.

3. Heat 3 Tbsp oil in a wok and brown garlic. Add chilli paste and stir-fry for a few seconds. Add prawns and stir-fry for a few seconds. Add noodles and toss well for a few minutes, then add Chinese chives and bean sprouts.

4. Combine thick sweet soy sauce, light soy sauce and sugar and stir well. Pour over ingredients in the wok and stir-fry for a few minutes. Push noodles to the side of the wok and add the remaining oil and eggs. Leave eggs to cook for 30 seconds, or until set, then scramble with noodles and bean sprouts. Sprinkle over some water and toss well. Lastly add cockles and stir-fry for a few seconds. Serve immediately with a dash of pepper.

SINGAPORE FRIED KWAY TEOW

Singapore fried kway teow is similar to Penang fried *kway teow* as they are both slightly sweet, but the Singapore dish has Chinese flowering cabbage which I find to be a tasty addition and I never fail to have it at least once whenever I am in Singapore. For this dish, use the firmer variety of *kway teow*, as the softer variety is more suitable to use in soups. Rinsing and scalding the noodles before cooking gets rid of excess oil. The cockles can be pried open easily and removed with a small sharp knife. Discard the droplet of mud in the cockles. If you find this difficult, scald the cockles in hot water for 15 seconds before removing. The cockle flesh will also be slightly cooked.

Preparation Time: 15 minutes
Cooking Time: 10 minutes
Serves 2

Cooking oil 2¹/₂ Tbsp

Garlic 2 cloves, peeled and chopped

Fresh flat rice noodles 140 g (5 oz), rinsed in warm water, drained and rinsed in tap water

Fresh yellow noodles 55 g (2 oz), scalded in hot water

Light soy sauce 2 Tbsp

Thick sweet soy sauce (*kicap manis*) 1 tsp

Egg 1, beaten with a pinch of pepper

Bean sprouts 55 g (2 oz), tails removed

Water 1–2 Tbsp

Cockles 70 g (2¹/₂ oz)

Hong Kong mustard greens 3–5 stalks, cut into 4-cm (1¹/₂-in) lengths

Salt ¹/₂ tsp

Sugar ¹/₂ tsp

Anchovies (*ikan bilis*) 1 Tbsp, fried

Chilli Paste

Red chillies 4, seeded and cut into 2.5-cm (1-in) pieces

Bird's eye chillies (*cili padi*) 6, seeded

Shallots 4, peeled

Salt 1 tsp

Sugar 1 tsp

1. To prepare chilli paste, combine red chillies, bird's eye chillies, shallots, salt and sugar in a food processor and blend until smooth. Set aside.

2. Heat 2 Tbsp oil in a wok and brown garlic. Add chilli paste and stir-fry for a few seconds or until fragrant. Add rice noodles and stir-fry for a few minutes, then add yellow noodles and continue cooking until heated through.

3. Combine light soy sauce and thick sweet soy sauce and stir well. Pour over ingredients in the wok and toss well. Push noodles to one side of the wok and add 1 tsp oil in the centre. Pour in beaten egg. Allow to set then scramble and mix with the noodles. Add bean sprouts and water and stir-fry for a few seconds. Lastly add cockles. Toss for a couple of seconds. Transfer noodles to a serving dish.

4. Meanwhile, boil a pot of water and add the remaining oil, salt and sugar. Scald Hong Kong mustard greens. Drain well and place on top of noodles. Top with fried anchovies and serve immediately.

THAI-STYLE FRIED NOODLES PHAD THAI

This famous Thai noodles is similar to Singapore and Malaysian fried *kway teow* cooked with distinctive Thai flavours.

Preparation Time: 20 minutes
Cooking Time: 20 minutes
Serves 4

Shelled small prawns (shrimps) 20

Salt $1/2$ tsp

Ground white pepper $1/4$ tsp

Cooking oil 3 Tbsp

Shallots 3, peeled and sliced

Garlic 4 cloves, peeled and minced

Preserved radish (*chai poh*) 45 g (1$1/2$ oz), rinsed and finely chopped

Dried chillies 20, seeded, soaked, ground and seasoned with 2 tsp salt and $1/4$ tsp pepper

Firm bean curd 1 piece, diced

Eggs 4, lightly beaten with $1/4$ tsp salt and $1/4$ tsp pepper

Fresh flat rice noodles 500 g (1 lb 1$1/2$ oz)

Bean sprouts 200 g (7 oz), tails removed

Chinese chives 55 g (2 oz), cut into 5-cm (2-in) lengths

Dried prawns (shrimps) 3 Tbsp, rinsed, coarsely ground and pan-fried dry

Fried peanuts 2 Tbsp, coarsely ground

Spring onions (scallions) 2 Tbsp chopped

Sauce

Water 180 ml (6 fl oz / $3/4$ cup)

Palm sugar (*gula melaka*) 55 g (2 oz), chopped

Tamarind pulp 1 Tbsp, mixed with 6 Tbsp water and strained

Fish sauce 1 Tbsp

Light soy sauce 1 Tbsp

1. To make sauce, combine water, palm sugar, tamarind juice, fish sauce and light soy sauce in a small saucepan. Bring to the boil and stir well until palm sugar dissolves. Reserve 6 Tbsp for use and store the remainder for future use. It will keep for 2 weeks refrigerated and longer if frozen.

2. Season prawns with salt and pepper. Set aside.

3. Heat 2$1/2$ Tbsp oil in a wok and brown shallots and garlic. Add preserved radish and stir-fry for a few minutes or until fragrant. Add dried chilli mixture and stir-fry for a few minutes. Add prawns and bean curd, and continue to cook for a few minutes. Push fried ingredients to one side of the wok and heat the remaining oil in the wok. Pour in beaten eggs and allow to set slightly before stirring to break up the omelette.

4. Add noodles and stir-fry for a few seconds. Add bean sprouts, chives, dried prawns and peanuts and toss to mix well. Pour in reserved sauce, then add spring onions and stir-fry for a few minutes.

5. Divide noodles into individual plates and serve with chilli flakes, if desired.

CHICKEN SOUP MEE SUA WITH POACHED EGG

This makes a quick nourishing meal for one. Double the ingredients for this recipe to serve two.

Preparation Time: 10 minutes
Cooking Time: 10 minutes
Serves 1

Chicken fillet 55 g (2 oz), sliced

Salt 1/4 tsp

Ground white pepper 1/4 tsp

Fresh chicken stock (page 20) 250 ml (8 fl oz / 1 cup)

Enoki mushrooms 30 g (1 oz), rinsed

Tomato 1, quartered

Short-stem mustard greens or *kai lan* 2 stalks

Bean sprouts 30 g (1 oz), tails removed

Flour vermicelli (*mee sua*) 70 g (2 1/2 oz)

Egg 1

Spring onion (scallion) 1, chopped

Shallot crisps to garnish

1. Season chicken with salt and pepper. Set aside.

2. Boil stock in a pot. Add chicken, mushrooms and tomato. Allow to cook for a few minutes. Remove from heat and set aside.

3. Boil a pot of water and scald mustard greens or *kai lan*. Drain and set aside.

4. Reheat water and scald bean sprouts and noodles separately. Drain and set aside.

5. Place noodles and bean sprouts into a serving bowl. Pour over soup and chicken, leaving enough stock in the pot to poach the egg.

6. Bring stock to a quick boil, drop in egg, cover and poach for a couple of minutes, or until egg is just done. Remove egg with a slotted spoon and place on top of noodles. Add mustard greens or *kai lan* and pour remaining stock over. Sprinkle over spring onions and shallot crisps. Serve immediately.

FRIED MEE SUA

Flour vermicelli (*mee sua*) is not easy to fry and requires quick and adept hands. You may have to do this several times before you are able to master it.

Preparation Time: 20 minutes
Cooking Time: 20 minutes
Serves 4

Cooking oil 750 ml (24 fl oz / 3 cups), for deep-frying

Flour vermicelli (*mee sua*) 280 g (10 oz)

Bean sprouts 450 g (1 lb), tails removed

Water 1.5 litres (48 fl oz / 6 cups)

Shallots 5, peeled and sliced

Garlic 4 cloves, peeled and minced

Chicken or pork 140 g (5 oz), cut into strips

Shelled small prawns (shrimps) 280 g (10 oz)

Salt 1 tsp

Ground white pepper 1 tsp

Fresh chicken or anchovy (*ikan bilis*) stock (page 20) 750 ml (24 fl oz / 3 cups)

Chinese flowering cabbage (*choy sum*) 4 stalks, cut into 5-cm (2-in) lengths

Light soy sauce 2 Tbsp

Spring onions (scallions) 2, sliced

Coriander leaves (cilantro) 2 sprigs

Red chillies 4, seeded and sliced

1. Heat oil in a wok until hot. Add vermicelli, a bundle at a time, and fry, turning over very quickly with chopsticks until golden. Vermicelli will sizzle in hot oil. Remove as soon as it stops sizzling. This takes only 15 seconds. Drain in a colander.

2. Remove oil, reserving 6 Tbsp. Heat half the reserved oil in a wok and add bean sprouts. Stir-fry for a few seconds. Dish out and leave aside.

3. Pour water into the wok and bring to the boil. Add fried vermicelli and stir-fry for a few minutes until soft. Immediately pour vermicelli into a colander and drain well.

4. Heat the remaining oil in a wok and brown shallots and garlic. Add chicken or pork and stir-fry for a few minutes, then add prawns, salt and pepper. Remove and set aside.

5. Pour chicken or anchovy stock into the wok and bring to the boil. Add Chinese flowering cabbage, stems first, then add light soy sauce and cook for a few minutes.

6. Add vermicelli, bean sprouts, fried meat and prawns and toss well. Top with spring onions and coriander leaves. Serve immediately with a saucer of sliced red chillies and light soy sauce.

BLACK PEPPER UDON

When this dish was first introduced in restaurants in Malaysia, it was a hit due to the different texture and flavour of the udon noodles, which was not easily available then. Today udon noodles can be obtained from most supermarkets.

Preparation Time: 15 minutes
Cooking Time: 15 minutes
Serves 4

Chicken thigh 1, skinned and shredded

Black peppercorns 1 tsp, coarsely crushed

Light soy sauce 1 tsp

Salt $1/2$ tsp

Sugar $1/2$ tsp

Udon 700 g (1 $1/2$ lb)

Cooking oil 2 Tbsp

Onion 1 medium, peeled and sliced

Garlic 3 cloves, peeled and chopped

Red chilli 1, seeded and chopped

Chinese cooking wine (Shaoxing) 1 tsp

Chinese cabbage 5 leaves, cut into 1-cm ($1/2$-in) strips

Chinese chives 6 stalks, cut into 2.5-cm (1-in) lengths

Corn flour (cornstarch) 1 tsp, mixed with 2 Tbsp water

Spring onions (scallion) 2, chopped

Coriander leaves (cilantro) 3 sprigs, chopped

Sauce

Fresh chicken stock (page 20) 180 ml (6 fl oz / $3/4$ cup)

Oyster sauce 1 Tbsp

Light soy sauce 1 Tbsp

Dark soy sauce $1/2$ Tbsp

Sugar $1/2$ tsp

Ground black pepper $1/4$ tsp

Salt $1/2$ tsp

1. Season chicken with crushed peppercorns, light soy sauce, salt and sugar. Set aside.

2. Boil a large pot of water and scald noodles for a few seconds. Drain and set aside.

3. Heat oil in a wok and fry onion until transparent. Add garlic and chilli and stir-fry until golden, then add chicken.

4. Add wine, then Chinese cabbage and stir-fry for 1 minute.

5. Combine sauce ingredients and stir well. Pour into a pot and bring to the boil. Add noodles and toss well. Cover wok and allow noodles to cook for a few minutes.

6. Remove cover and stir in chives. Add corn flour mixture to thicken sauce. Divide noodles into individual serving bowls and garnish with spring onions and coriander leaves. Serve immediately.

COLD GREEN TEA SOBA

Soba noodles can be served hot or cold. Most connoisseurs prefer it cold. Do not be misled by the simplicity of the dish. Although simple, it is very tasty noodle dish and I have yet to come across anyone who does not like it.

Preparation Time: 15 minutes
Cooking Time: 15 minutes
Serves 4

Onion 1, peeled and thinly sliced

Cold water 500 ml (16 fl oz / 2 cups)

Salt $^1/_2$ tsp

Green tea soba 200 g (7 oz)

Wakame 15 g ($^1/_2$ oz), soaked for 10 minutes

Pea shoots (*dou miao*) 55 g (2 oz)

Dressing

Japanese soy sauce 2 Tbsp

Olive oil 2 Tbsp

Lemon juice 1 Tbsp

1. Combine onion and cold water in a small bowl. Stir in salt and chill in the refrigerator.

2. Boil a pot of water and cook noodles for 4–5 minutes. Drain and plunge into a basin of cold water. Strain noodles and set aside in the refrigerator.

3. Reheat water and scald wakame for a few minutes to soften. Drain and shred into 1-cm ($^1/_2$-in) thick strips. Set aside in the refrigerator.

4. Reheat water and scald pea shoots for a few seconds in seasoned water. Drain and set aside in the refrigerator.

5. Place noodles, wakame, onion and pea shoots on a serving plate. Combine Japanese soy sauce, olive oil and lemon juice and stir well. Pour over noodles, toss well and serve immediately.

MUSHROOM UDON SOUP

This healthy Japanese noodle dish is easy to prepare and very delicious.
It's always a favourite with my friends when they want a simple and light meal.

Preparation Time: 10 minutes
Cooking Time: 10 minutes
Serves 4

Chicken fillet 85 g (3 oz)

Salt 1/2 tsp

Instant dashi 18 g (1/2 oz)

Water 1.25 litres (40 fl oz / 5 cups)

Japanese soy sauce 2 Tbsp

Mirin 2 Tbsp

Hon shimeji mushrooms 140 g (5 oz), trimmed and rinsed

Leek 55 g (2 oz), thinly sliced

Udon 400 g (14 1/3 oz)

Eggs 4

Spring onions (scallions) 2, chopped

Nori 5-cm (2-in), shredded

1. Season chicken with salt and set aside.

2. Combine dashi and water in a large pot and bring to the boil. Add Japanese soy sauce, mirin and chicken, cover and allow stock to come to the boil. Add mushrooms and leek. Remove from heat and set aside.

3. Meanwhile, boil a pot of water and scald noodles for a few minutes or until just cooked through. Drain and set aside.

4. Drain three-quarters of the boiling water from the pot. Break egg, one at a time, into a small bowl and drop into the pot of boiling water. Poach eggs for a few seconds or until egg white is opaque and the yolk is still runny.

5. Divide noodles into individual serving bowls and top each bowl with a poached egg. Pour dashi stock over. Garnish with spring onions and nori. Serve immediately.

GLOSSARY

NOODLES

Board Noodles

Known as *pan mee* in Hokkien, these flat noodles are made from wheat flour, water, salt and eggs. It is usually served in soup or tossed in a soy sauce mixture. These noodles are freshly made and do not contain preservatives or colouring.

Egg Noodles

Made from wheat flour, eggs and water, egg noodles have a bright yellow colour and rich flavour. Egg noodles are also known as *wanton mee* in Hokkien. They vary in threadlike broadness and are also available in flat broad strips. Egg noodles are available fresh or dried. Fresh noodles keep well in sealed plastic containers or bags in the refrigerator. They can also be frozen for longer storage. A recipe for fresh egg noodles can be found on page 14.

Egg Noodle Sticks

Made from enriched wheat flour and eggs, these noodles come in flat sticks measuring 20-cm (8-in) in length. They are sold in supermarkets and Chinese grocery stores in flat packets.

Flat Rice Noodles

Flat rice noodles are also known as *kway teow* in Cantonese and Hokkien. They are made from rice ground with water, and then steamed into thin sheets. The sheets are then rolled up and sliced in varying widths. Flat rice noodles are available fresh and dried from the supermarkets and markets. Flat rice noodles will keep refrigerated for up to 3 days.

Flour Vermicelli

Known as *mee sua* in Hokkien or *meen seen* in Cantonese, the name literally means "thread noodles". It is made from unbleached wheat flour. The thinner variety is usually used in soups and the thicker one used for frying.

Fresh Yellow Noodles

Known as *mee* in Hokkien and *meen* in Cantonese, fresh yellow noodles are made from flour, water, alkaline water and yellow food colouring. They come in small, medium and thick strands and can be stir-fried, braised or boiled in soups. Fresh yellow noodles will keep well stored in an air-tight container or sealed plastic bags for a week in the refrigerator or several weeks in the freezer. A recipe for fresh yellow noodles can be found on page 12.

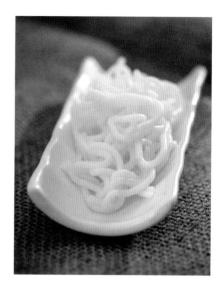

Mouse-tail Noodles

Also known as *loh shee fun* in Cantonese, these are short fat rice noodles, about 4-cm (1^3/$_4$-in) in length, mouse-tail noodles are easily available fresh in supermarkets and wet markets.

Pre-fried Egg Noodles

Known as *yee mee* in Hokkien, these noodles are sold pre-fried in large round cakes, usually 3–4 cakes in a pack. They have to be briefly scalded in boiling water before use.

Fresh Thick Rice Noodles

These thick white strands of noodles are made from rice. They are available fresh or dried. Fresh rice noodles keep for only 2–3 days. Dried rice noodles have to be scalded to soften before use.

Dried Fine Rice Vermicelli

Known as *bee hoon* in Hokkien and *mai fun* in Cantonese, rice vermicelli is made from ground rice and come in a variety of thickness. These dried noodles have a long shelf life and therefore make a good store ingredient. Dried rice vermicelli has to be soaked in water or scalded and drained quickly to soften before use.

Soba

A Japanese noodle made from buckwheat and wheat flour, soba has a chewy texture and nutty aroma. Buckwheat flour has no gluten and is dark in colour which explains the dark colour of the soba noodle. Soba is available in several varieties flavoured with black sesame seeds or green tea. It is rich in protein and is said to help lower blood pressure. Soba is known to have a high dietary fibre content that can help improve digestive and bowel activity.

Transparent Vermicelli

Also known as glass noodles, bean thread noodles or cellophane noodles, transparent vermicelli is only available in dried form. Made from mung beans, this versatile noodle can be served in soups, braised or fried. Soak in water for 10–15 minutes to soften before use.

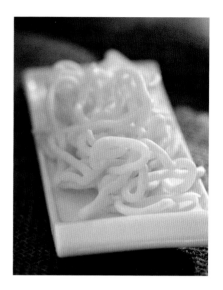

Udon

These thick round white noodles are made from wheat. They are easy to use and come ready-cooked in packets.

Anchovies (*Ikan Bilis*)

These small dried fish range from 2.5–5-cm (1–2-in) in length. They are often fried and made into sambal or mixed with fried peanuts and served with *nasi lemak* or porridge. They are also used to make stock. The heads and entrails should be removed and the fish rinsed before use. A recipe for anchovy (*ikan bilis*) stock can be found on page 20.

Chilli Oil

Chilli oil is used extensively in Sichuan cooking. To make chilli oil, soak about 20 dried chillies in hot water until soft. Remove seeds, if a less spicy oil is preferred. Place softened chillies in a blender with about 150 ml (5 fl oz / $^2/_3$ cup) cooking oil. Blend mixture coarsely and pour into a small saucepan. Cook over low heat for 3–5 minutes. Strain, cool and store in a glass jar in a cool place. Chilli oil will keep indefinitely.

Coconut Cream (*Pati Santan*)

Thick fresh coconut cream obtained without adding water. It can be diluted with any amount of water as required to make thin or coconut cream. Coconut cream keeps well for up to 2 weeks frozen in plastic bags or sealed containers.

Dried Chinese Mushrooms

There are many varieties of dried Chinese mushrooms but the larger ones with a cracked surface offer the best flavour and bite. To prepare them, soak them in a bowl of water for 20–30 minutes until they are soft, then pliable. Squeeze out the excess water and discard the woody stems. Use as required in the recipe. Dried Chinese mushrooms should be stored in an air-tight jar in a cool place.

Dried Sour Fruit (*Asam Gelugor*)

These dried sour fruit slices are made from the ripe fruit of the *asam gelugor* tree. They are usually added to curries and soups are used for flavouring fish.

Galangal

This rhizome looks like ginger, but it can be distinguished by its faint pinkish colour. Galangal has a delicate flavour is used normally fresh in curries and hot soups.

Ground Chilli Paste (*Cili Boh*)

This chilli paste is made by blending softened dried chillies with water. Although it is available commercially, making your own is simple and easy. Wash and soak approximately 12 dried chillies. If a less fiery paste is preferred, remove the seeds by cutting the chillies and shaking the seeds out. Place in a blender with 3–4 Tbsp water and puree into a fine paste. Store refrigerated in an air-tight jar.

Kaffir Lime and Kaffir Lime Leaves

Kaffir lime is a round, often knobbly, green citrus fruit. The rind is commonly used for its sharp bitter sweet taste. Added to curries, it imparts a fragrant lemony flavour.

Leaves of the kaffir lime tree are also referred to as "double lime leaves", because of its shape which looks like two leaves joined together. Its special fragrance is specially favoured to use in curries. Tear or finely shred them to release the distinctive flavour.

Lemongrass

A long grass with a pale yellow thick stem, the lemongrass imparts delicate fragrance and flavour to Asian curries and soups. Usually, only the lower root end is used, either bruised or sliced.

Laksa Leaves (*Daun Kesom*)

Also known as Vietnamese mint, laksa leaves have a pungent flavour and should be used sparingly. It is an essential ingredient in spicy noodle soups like laksa and curries.

Pickled Garlic Stems (*Tang Chai*)

Pickled garlic stems are sold in round earthen jars or in plastic packs. It is a Teochew favourite, mainly used in soups. To prepare for use, rinse in several changes of water and squeeze dry.

Pickled Garlic

Pickled garlic is a Thai product. It is sold in jars and is available from supermarkets. Pickled garlic is made using the Thai garlic, which is smaller than the common garlic. It can be used as a seasoning, sliced or whole in salads and curries.

Potato Flour

Like corn flour, potato flour can be used as a thickening agent. It is more gelatinous than corn flour and gives a more subtle shiny finish to sauces. It can be substituted with tapioca or corn flour but use only two-thirds the quantity if doing so.

Sesame Paste

A thick aromatic paste of ground sesame seeds. When using sesame paste fresh from the jar, stir it to mix it with the layer of oil and thin it with some water if necessary. Sesame paste is available from Chinese grocery stores. If unavailable, smooth peanut butter can be used as a substitute.

Tamarind Pulp

This rich brown pulp from the tamarind
fruit often contain seeds and fibre. To
obtain tamarind juice, soak in water and
strain the pulp. This fragrant sourish
juice is typically used to flavour curries
and sambals.

Torch Ginger Buds
(*Bunga Kantan*)

This pretty pink flower bud of the torch
ginger plant is deeply aromatic when
harvested before it blooms. The entire
flower bud from the outer petals to
the inner bud and stem can be used
to flavour curries, sambals and soups in
Asian cooking.

INDEX